I0100634

NARRATIVE WORLDVIEWS OF CENTRAL AMERICAN MIGRATION

A MULTI-VANTAGE APPROACH

NARRATIVE WORLDVIEWS OF CENTRAL AMERICAN MIGRATION:

A MULTI-VANTAGE APPROACH

JARED JOHNSON
SKYE COOLEY
ASYA COOLEY
ROBERT HINCK

COMMON GROUND

First published in 2024
as part of the Gobal Studies Book Imprint
doi: 10.18848/978-1-963049-31-2/CGP (Full Book)

Common Ground Research Networks
University of Illinois Research Park
2001 South First St, Suite 201 L
Champaign, IL 61820 USA

Copyright © Johnson, Jared; Cooley, Skye C.; Cooley, Asya Besova; Hinck, Robert S.,

All rights reserved. Apart from fair dealing for the purposes of study, research, criticism or review as permitted under the applicable copyright legislation, no part of this book may be reproduced by any process without written permission from the publisher.

Library of Congress Cataloging-in-Publication Data

Names: Johnson, Jared, author, Cooley, Skye C., author, Cooley, Asya Besova, author, Hinck, Robert S., author.
Title: Narrative worldviews of Central American migration : a multi-vantage approach / Jared Johnson, Skye Cooley, Asya Cooley, Robert Hinck.

Description: Champaign, IL : Common Ground Research Networks, 2024. Includes bibliographical references and index. | Summary: "The perspectives offered in this work come from 40 interviews with migrants, law enforcement officers, journalists, film-makers, policy experts, vocational workers, shelter workers, migration lawyers, missionaries, academics, and non-profits; people from the NT region, people from the US, people in the ivory tower and those who put their lives very much at risk on the ground. The work also examines 50,000+ news media articles from the US, Mexico, and the NT and over 50 policy briefs detailing challenges and possible solutions to mass irregular migration. The data collected cuts across political and economic borders in order to map out a comprehensive set of narratives addressing migration holistically. A unique aspect of the data is the inclusion of policy data in the analysis as its own distinct narrative vantage. It is our hope that the book informs better policies that help build more vibrancy and safety throughout the Americas"-- Provided by publisher.

Identifiers: LCCN 2024012990 (print) | LCCN 2024012991 (ebook) | ISBN 9781963049299 (hardback) | ISBN 9781963049305 (paperback) | ISBN 9781963049312 (pdf)
Subjects: LCSH: Immigrants--Central America. | Central America--Emigration and immigration--Attitudes.
Classification: LCC JV7412 .J64 2024 (print) | LCC JV7412 (ebook) | DDC 305.9/0691209728--dc23/eng/20240501

LC record available at https://lccn.loc.gov/2024012990
LC ebook record available at https://lccn.loc.gov/2024012991

Cover Design Credit: Phillip Kalantzis Cope
Cover Photo Credit: Joseph Sorrentino (La Patrona, Veracruz/Mexico-February, 2012. An 11 year old Honduran riding the freight train they call La Bestia) Licence Purchased on Shutterstock.

TABLE OF CONTENTS

Chapter 1: Introduction   1

Chapter 2: Methods   19

- Stakeholder Interviews   19

- News Media Coverage   22

- Policy Briefs   26

- Triangulating Narratives across Interview and News Media Data   28

Chapter 3: In-Depth Interviews   33

- Themes within Sense-Making Claims   34

- Themes within Exclusion–Inclusion Claims   43

- Phenomena of Interest   55

- Additional Themes and Conclusions   60

Chapter 4: News Media, Narrative Divergence   63

- Method   66

- Mexican Media Narratives   67

- NT Media Narratives   78

- US Media Narratives   88

- Discussion   101

Chapter 5: Triangulating News Media   109

- Method   111

- Findings   111

- Discussion   121

Chapter 6: Policy Briefs   129

- Themes within Sense-Making Claims   130

- Themes within Exclusion–Inclusion Claims   135

- Phenomenon of Interest   140
- Conclusions/Recommendations   145

Chapter 7: Narrative Alignment   159

- Narrative Alignment 1: Migrants Are Seeking a Better Life   160
- Narrative Alignment 2: The Migration Journey Is Perilous   161
- Narrative Alignment 3: The US Migration Infrastructure and
  Policy Have Not Been Able to Either Deter Migration or
  Facilitate Efficient Legal Migration   162

Conclusions: Key Elements of the Northern Triangle Migration Narrative 163

## CHAPTER 1

Introduction

The first quarter of the 21st century has come with a litany of crises, conflicts, and backsliding of democratic control of the global order (Hyde, 2020), the culmination of which exposes genuine existential threats to modern human societies, as evidenced by the simultaneously ongoing Holocene extinction event and largest forcibly displaced population ever recorded in human history. While differing catalysts and provocations, often rooted in economic-based resource extraction and the widening of historical social power imbalances, are easily blamed for the failures of an emergent global society to address these mounting challenges, what can no longer be ignored is that non-causal failures, namely, an inability to co-create shared meaning and find common perspective in the moment, are major contributing factors (Cooley et al., 2022).

It is paradoxically startling that a failure to create shared meaning socially should so evidentially manifest in an era literally defined by the global interconnectivity of our species. That near limitless information availability and expansive connectivity into a networked society has not alleviated basic out-grouping mistrust or promoted universal welfare initiatives is explicable only when we recognize that human beings are not primarily rational agents acting on objective truths (Killingsworth & Gilbert, 2010). Instead, we are instinctually and emotively driven (Bechara et al., 2000) toward evolutionary fitness (Hoffman & Prakash, 2014). The shortcuts and heuristics of our evolutionary attunement necessarily blind us to certain aspects of the incessant flow of phenomena constantly barraging our senses, as well as to the impacts our actions have on the greater surrounding environment, as a matter of efficiency to pursue partners and secure resources. These patterns of efficiency become codified as system knowledge, theory, and culture and themselves fundamentally inhibit how individuals and societies can imagine outcomes in the world (Swanson, 2016). That is, irrespective of the quality or quantity of information, an individual, or society, can only make use of that information to the extent of its theoretical understandings of reality, which are limited by ontological identities (Beckett & Morris, 2001) bounded by the confines of evolutionary attunement. Thus, how we impact the environment is very much limited by our worldviews and assumed environmental knowledge.

Perhaps even more insightful is that when systems, and individuals, face uncertainties, they do so as a challenge of ontological security (Mitzen, 2006); meaning that every question of survival is foundationally also a question of the validity of held worldviews and assumed knowledge. Rather than abandoning, or even modifying, the successful evolutionary pathways we have inherited from our social constructions of reality (which lack the conference of full objective truth), our efficient-focused brains hardwire preference to the known as an evolutionary default (Polansky & Rieger, 2020), locking us in a mindset of protectionism that escalatory-entrenches when facing scrutiny (Galef, 2010). This tendency of entrenchment is actually made easier by an overabundance of available information. As specific-selection of information is required on any given subject, selection preferences seek and filter new information through a confirmatory lens (Del Vicario et al., 2017); creating hyper-polarizing and niche-driven population segmentation. The need to find a common vantage from which to evaluate, discuss, and solve destabilization at global scales is evident and possible through shared narrative. The evidence for and utility of such common narratives are presented here in the context of mass migration of Central Americans to North America.

The research offered provides numerous vantages of various flashpoints concerning migration from the so-called Northern Triangle (NT) of Guatemala, El Salvador, and Honduras. This complex issue can be viewed from various arenas, including causes of the forced migration, attempts to address the causes, the challenges migrants face in their migratory journey, and, ultimately, the process of resettlement (legally or otherwise) in their ultimate destination. The idea is that the stories told about events present a framework of understanding representative of worldview, virtue, and sense of purpose. The stories encapsulate impact and effectiveness of various policies, a more complete extent of the humanitarian crisis, and ways in which policies can help or hinder the crisis. By coalescing stories from different cultures and vantages, on the same topic, a larger image unfolds where alignments and misalignments of interest can be more clearly seen. Each story is its own map outlining an observed external reality in varying gradients of agreement with others. Here, aligning these stories presents a larger picture of the scope of migration's challenges, one that forces reimagination of common narrative, and subsequently how nation-state struc-tures can more intentionally interact in modernity.

The vantages offered in this work come from forty interviews with migrants, law enforcement officers, journalists, filmmakers, policy experts, vocation-al workers, shelter workers, migration lawyers, missionaries, academics, and non-profits; people from the NT region, people from the US, people in the ivory tower, and those who put their lives very much at risk on the ground. The work also examined more than 50,000 news media articles from the US, Mexico, and the NT, as well as over fifty policy briefs detailing challenges and possible solutions to mass irregular migration. The data collected cuts across political and economic borders in order to map out a comprehensive set of narratives. A unique aspect of the data is the inclusion of policy data in the analysis, as its own distinct narrative vantage.

Building a Macro-Narrative-Based Assessment of Migration Policy

Narratives within politics are tools wielded by political operatives to achieve particular objectives contextualized to an issue, political body, and cultural cli-mate; policy narratives thus simultaneously provide multiple layers of interpre-tive function (McBeth et al., 2014). Evaluations of narrative policy frameworks identify micro, meso, and macro vantages, arguing that to fully understand the meso and macro levels of policy narratives, the micro individual level must also be understood (McBeth et al, 2014). The inclusion of policy narratives in this study attempts to fulfill the need to comprehend policy, particularly within Central American migration issues at the individual level of both stakeholder and migrant.

Our project follows Daiute and Nelson's sense-making notion of narrative in that the function of narrative is an expression of self-awareness within the con-text of one's own cultural experience and personal history (Daiute & Nelson, 1997). In such light, narrative is seen as an insight into the "landscape of con-sciousness" of the narrator, giving contextual links to point of view, interpreta-tion of sequential events, and sense-making of action. The ordering of events in an environment is argued as relationally bound, motivating questions, such as "what will happen next," "where do I fit in," "what is happening," that demand narrative responses based on cultural scripts and individual vantage points

(Daiute & Nelson, 1997, p. 209). Cultural scripts implicitly embed beliefs, values, and expectations of culture into sense-making, while personal vantage points and evaluations assist in distinguishing self from other. Importantly, access to a variety of cultural scripts from which to assess personal vantage allows for broader interpretive functions. The project attempts a response to calls for a need in narrative-based understandings of migration (Dennison, 2021).

Much research has been conducted on individual areas of migration. Economic models for integrating migrants (Stenis, 2020) and social integration accelerants of migration (Waldorf, 2018) focus on practical networking and instrumentation when discussing improvements to migration. Research on policy-making suggests narrative plays a key role in sense-making (Crow & Lawlor, 2016), specifically in migration policy, by shaping how audiences makes sense of public support and sentiment (Slaven & Boswell, 2019; Steinhilper & Gruijters, 2018). Media coverage thus plays an important role by providing factual data from which migration policies can be deliberated (Aalberg & Beyer, 2015; Benson & Wood, 2015; Blinder & Allen, 2016; Hallin, 2015; Thorbjørnsrud, 2015). However, research has also shown a divide between factual data, public opinion, and news coverage of migration (Harris & Gruenewald, 2020). Such divides represent, as is argued in this study, a lack of individual and culturally grounded vantages from which the public can construct a sensible macro-narrative on the issue and its policies. That is, public opinion on the issue of migration and its policies are informed largely by narrow silos of information, potentially divorced from a larger reality; policy is thus judged as politically contrived in service to a nuanced land of illusion. Specifically, studies show linkages of migration to crime (Collingwood & O'Brien Gonzalez, 2019), as well as broad negative and detrimental media frames of migrants (Farris & Silber Mohamed, 2018; Innes, 2010).

Media frames are shown as coalescing stereotyped visions of migrants (Greussing & Boomgaarden, 2017), predominately focused on short-term, elite-driven tactical descriptions. National media from around the world depict migrants as economic opportunity seekers, terrorists, asylum seekers, and threats to state interest (Farris & Silber Mohamed, 2018; Innes, 2010). The predominate cultural scripts present migrants as anonymous objects linked to crime, threat, and danger (Gabrielatos & Baker, 2008; Horsti, 2008). Studies show that media reporting influences public opinion and policy related to how to treat migrants (Blinder & Allen, 2016; Hallin, 2015), including the use of metaphors characterizing migrants as unclean pollutants of society (Cisneros, 2008). Irregular migrants have been shown as one of the most marginalized groups in Western societies, with their negative portrayals in media contributing to their dehumanization (Esses et al., 2013).

Studies critiquing media coverage of migrants argue there is a lack of focus on systemic and structural factors necessary for a more complete public understanding of migration policies (Benson, 2013; Suro, 2008), as well as noting a lack of empirical descriptions exploring how migration media coverage has shifted over time (Harris & Gruenewald, 2020). Further, studies on migration focus attention largely on host nation national media coverage (Palau-Sampio, 2019), highlighting only one dimension of a multidimensional problem contextualized primarily as concerns of the nation state (Cooley et al., 2022). Thus the ability to synthesize the transnational nature of migratory issues and policies faces a multitude of constraints, stemming largely from tactical-event–oriented national cultural scripts from media and isolated individual perspectives of migration hindered by experience, media stereotypes, and political contrivances. Indeed, even narrative-based policy research on migration often examines only particular events or issues, such as border deaths (Steinhilper & Gruijters, 2018), US–Mexican policy alignment (Alba, 2021), key frameworks, and the assessment of national risk (Lawlor & Crow, 2018), and largely comes as a self-contained examination of solely policy narratives themselves (Crow & Jones, 2018).

The primary data assessed in this project provides both cultural scripts and individual vantages from news media and in-depth interviews. News media narrative analysis offers the cultural scripts of the state, while stakeholder and migrant interviews offer numerous individual vantages from which to view Central American migration. By providing wide-ranging narratives and vantages from which to view Central American migration, a more macro-narration of migration policy impacts is given. As a result, policy narratives can be more broadly understood. The unique contribution of this research is that it offers a variety of both cultural and individually vantaged perspectives from which to form a macro-narration of migration policy.

Limited Cultural Scripts—Social Contracts and the Exclusion of Migrants

The movement of people across the planet in search of hope, opportunity, and safety is a natural and historic process as old as our species. The imposition of societal-based property laws necessary for sustained securement of resources, as well as the conceptualization of citizenship and territorial sovereignty, are likewise the historical and evolutionary human responses toward managing this otherwise unmitigated movement of people. While the fixedness of man-made territorialism may wane depending on factors such as war, economic (inter) dependence, and like-mindedness of cultural ideologies, the expansive application of Westphalian notions of statehood have underpinned how migration-related laws have developed; rather than enforcement by bondage, modern states restrict the movement of people via exclusion (Bauder, 2018). Thus, it is unsurprising that migrants have historically been wielded as both political tools and scapegoats by nation states, with more recent weaponizing of mass migration in US politics (Mousin, 2019) and hybrid warfare on the European continent (Sytas & Plucinska, 2021).

Exclusion, as such, is fueled by inculcated cultural scripts informing attitudes and practices that limit participation of foreigners in ways that explain their presence as possible enemies of the collective state (Dal Lago, 2009), i.e., outsiders. That is, social contracts are ontological in nature, demarcating the self in categorically segregating associations with others as the criteria for inclusion. While the nation state is most certainly an artificial construct, its design is rooted in the psychological need to maintain a discernibly predictable ordering of the environment. That nationalism and traditionalism take on their most vicious and virulent forms in times of great societal pressure and upheaval is explicable as a limit of imaginable outcomes allowable by cultural scripts bound by territorially based social contracts. Our models wed our conceivable questions, and therefore derivative outcomes, to the known (Kuhn, 2012). As existential challenges to the nation state arise, the search for solutions is restricted to the parameters of the state itself, inherently breeding the polarities of fundamentalist and progressivist interpretations of established state-centric policies. It is important to note here that imagination is linked to narrative accessibility (Dennison, 2021).

That the explosive rise of the human population is interlinked to our interconnectivity and ability to share knowledge is unsurprising. That the basis to that interconnectivity is economic trade and resource acquisition filtered through nation-state identities is noteworthy, however, as resource possession becomes a central aspect in defining the inclusion and exclusion criteria within cultural scripts. The intermarriage of the nation state to individual perception of possession thus unites resource acquisition to identity in profound ways. It has been noted that one can more easily imagine the end of the world than the end of capitalism (Green, 2020). That is, it is easier to ignore existential realities of man-made global destruction and staggering human inequality than to reimage the systems producing them, in part because this requires a reevaluation of national, and therefore self, identities. Our narratives limit our imaginable outcomes.

As one consequence of this lack in imagination, over seventy-nine million human beings are displaced globally, and over twenty-six million are defined as refugees, i.e., the excluded. Entire nations are defined by labels indicating their lack of prosperity, such as those referenced by a former US president as "shitholes" (Hitchcok, 2023). The instability and volatility that inclusion–exclusion criteria, based on resource possession afforded by nation-centric cultural scripts, has wrought in an era of hyper-mobility, globalized information sharing, and an unprecedently dense human population is startling. The complex challenges posed by massive populations of displaced people around the world, bound by the exclusion criteria of nation states, are difficult to conceptualize because solutions involve challenges to the understood manner in which the nation state fulfills obligations to those defined within the social contract as included. Devising solutions to challenges from within the systems producing them is rife with challenges. Thus, "irregular" migration provides a stark case study of the failures to imagine cooperative solutions beyond the confines of national cultural scripts designed to provide resources to those codified as included within their social contracts. *The hope in this work is that identifying culturally scripted and individually vantaged perspectives in narrative from a broad selection of data and stakeholders can uncover common interpretive perspectives on migration otherwise left in cultural or individual isolation.*

An Elusive Transnational Narrative of Migration

Narratives, although often evoked and constructed by policy makers and communicators, are rarely considered for what they are; how they are formed; how their popularities vary; their beginning and end points; and their effects on attitudes, behaviors, and policies, specifically, when discussing migration (Dennison, 2021). Despite an emergence of research applying narrative theory to macro-political inquiries, the study of political narratives is very much in its infancy (Shenhav, 2005). This is particularly true for migration research applying narrative theory (Dennison, 2021).

Dennison argues that there are a number of key features relevant to applying narrative analysis: (1) the formation and selection of narrative is inescapable, as they are necessary to organize and prioritize an amount of information that would otherwise overwhelm; (2) the utility of any narrative rests in its generalizability to multiple situations, adaptability is functionality; (3) narratives are distinct from frames and discourses, as broader orientations and trajectories. (4) narratives contain implicit and explicit normative contexts; (5) the potential number of narratives is limitless, but only a few gain popularity, restricting imaginative capacities (Dennison, 2021).

Narratives serve to group together, and sensibly integrate, a multitude of sensory experiences and recalled events; their organization function is a cognitive capacity limited by the human organism against an infinite reality (Ricoeur, 1984). Thus, narratives apply a filter to reality that prioritizes and rewards certain parameters and trajectories for an individual to pursue. While necessarily limiting, narrative sense-making of the environment nevertheless represents the macro for the individual. Which narratives are applied, and available, in given circumstances thus becomes extremely important in social contexts. The power of narrative is to set the terms of debate socially (Dennison, 2021), the power to determine who is the hero, the villain, the victim, the timekeeper (Jones, 2010). Anyone who has ever played make-believe with a child has experienced the power of narrative to shape the reality of events.

Researchers have argued that narratives are useful in understanding how policies can be adopted despite lacking reasoned debates (Sconfienza, 2017), as well as the limited perspective policy narratives necessarily take (Shenhav, 2006). Politically, narratives present a confluence of poorly linked and distorted causal factors to target actions toward (Dennison, 2021). Narrative binds selective histories, fiction and non-fiction, so that otherwise illogical actions may be considered appropriate (Wilson, 2005).

Recalling that the utility of narrative is in its generalizability (Shanahan et al., 2011), the implicit application of this generalizability to the environment is in connecting two or more points in time, relating a series of phenomena in a particular time sequence (Ricoeur, 1980). The persuasive power of narrative is in defining the criteria of causality, linking two otherwise segregable phenomena (Prince, 1982). At their most simplistic, narratives contain at least three elements, (1) an initial state of affairs, (2) a phenomenon, (3) a subsequent state of affairs (Czarniawska, 1998). Although narratives may inform hypotheses, propaganda, and conspiracy theory, narratives are informal and normatively loaded stories that inform actions across a variety of applications (Dennison, 2021). Political narratives face the added complexity of informing actual actions of governments in the real world; that is, political narratives bind action in political logics that attempt a literal shaping of the present and future in reference to lessons of the past (Shenhav, 2006). Thus, the expressed beginning and end points of political narratives are extremely consequential to sense-making, as are the embedded normative assumptions.

Narratives are essentially causal pathways. Irrespective of the degree to which they are aligned with an objective, observable reality, their generalizability ultimately relates to the internal coherence, interests, and physiological and cultural contexts of the receiver to whom it is presented. Thus, narratives are the guarantors of ontological security (Hinck et al., 2021), in that they stabilize the assumptions necessary for decision-making in an uncertain and complex environment. Importantly, narratives can be recognizably inaccurate or recognizably misrepresentative, yet still relied on because they cannot be thought beyond (Roe, 1994). The linkage of narratives, and the constraints imposed by narrative on imagination, have been explored by researchers, who argue that increased human interconnectivity and the complexity of such interactions have made sense-making simultaneously more selective and unpredictable (Beck, 1992, 1998; Boswell et al., 2011; Dennison, 2021). That is, we have more interconnections and information access, yet the scope of our collective sense-making remains limited to the confines of individualized narrative access.

The popularity and accessibility of certain political narratives over others is linked to the salience of a given issue, a growing need to make sense of that issue, and the degree to which the complexity of the issue can be understood (Dennison, 2019; Dennison & Geddes, 2019). Further, as an issue remains on a political agenda over time, politicians face justifying their own actions and behavior concerning the issue, which is done through contrived narratives ultimately in service to a political identity rather than the issue itself (Boswell et al., 2011). The reliance on narrative to inform identity and relay ontological security becomes particularly noteworthy in political contexts. Although human beings are often presented as protective of identity to a fault (Galef, 2021) and predisposed, by efficiency, toward detrimental cognitive biases, these analyses overlook the importance of individual deduction when grafting new information into existing ontologies (Dennison, 2019). That is, the adoption of narrative is determined by its internal congruence, the degree to which it makes theoretical sense, and its external congruence, the degree to which its claims align with the real world (Lodge & Taber, 2005).

Critically, narratives are more likely to be believed when they activate the imagination (Oatley, 1995). To the degree that narratives are causal pathways, those pathways themselves are capable of imaginative reconstruction and re-formulation. Individuals have more difficulty imaging from narratives that are foreign to them, or misaligned with pre-existing conceptions of causal chains, often leading to feelings of distrust, disassociation, and rejection. Thus, although human beings actively seek new information and constantly update their under-standings of the world based on new information (Dennison & Geddes, 2019), such updates are restricted to imaginative functions bound by engrained and ac-cessible narratives. However, when new narratives affirm self-identity and on-tological security, they are more likely to be successful (Shanahan et al., 2011).

Political narratives, particularly those involving transnational issues, prove especially difficult for individuals to imagine new pathways and outcomes from. This is because, as has already been mentioned, political narratives have inherent rigidities related to the normative existence of the nation state itself and therefore an individual's identity as associated within the inclusion criteria of the state. Thus, while an endless array of actions could be potentially de-rived from narrative imaginings of American exceptionalism (Krebs, 2015), in practice such imaginings are limited by constraints of the state itself. That is, narratives informing identity do not function to dissolve themselves. Instead, individuals transport themselves within the unfolding narratives of most utility to them in the moment (Green & Brock, 2002), focusing their mental capacities toward envisioning themselves enacting certain roles and playing certain char-acters (Busselle & Bilandzic, 2008).

The degree to which an individual is susceptible to being fully transported into a specific, or singular, narrative varies depending on predisposition and the persuasive power of the narrative itself in context (Lee & Shin, 2014). What moderates susceptibility of ontological dependence on particular narratives includes a host of factors: the need to make sense of an issue, its alignment with interests, theoretical plausibility, engagement of metacognition and imagination, and quality of storytelling (Dennison & Geddes, 2019). Transportation of self into narrative is important, as it is ultimately a means to empathy and self-reflection. However, narrative transportation also entails accepting selective claims concerning the categories, relationships, and casual mechanisms of the environment. Critically, the persuasive power of narrative includes engaging imagination and metacognition. In this way, even non-sensical causalities can be linked within persuasive political narratives so long as the narratives relied on are deeply tied to ontology, as ontologically wed narratives can most readily spark the imagination.

Specific research on the advancement of narrative theory into policy analysis includes the narrative policy framework (NPF) designed to examine policy narratives and empirically study their impacts (Jones, 2010). The NPF has been utilized to show how the narratives that obscure truth and diverge from democratic norms can undermine confidence in democracy (Jones & McBeth, 2020). In migration research, Trump's rhetoric was used to examine the impacts of narrative justifications for the industry of migrant detention (Estrada et al., 2020). Narratives found to be associated with migrants have had policy impacts related to public safety, crime, terrorism, and broader narratives of invasion (Mamadouh, 2012; Stewart, 2012). A few studies have considered positive migration narratives focusing on cultural and economic enrichment, freedom of people to move, and global development (Dennison & Geddes, 2019). Further, few studies have conducted transnational perspectives on migration toward a federation approach depoliticizing migration (Akesson & Baaz, 2015; Pécoud, 2015), while fewer still have examined how migration narratives impact policy preferences (Dennison & Geddes, 2019).

This work attempts a transnational perspective applied as a sense-making tool, or grand narrator, of policy narratives concerning mass migration coming from the NT into Mexico and the US. The focus of the work is on demonstrating the beginning and end points, phenomena of interest, selectively included causal links, and contexts within the narratives explored. Of particular importance is the comparison of cultural (i.e., news media data) and individual (i.e., interview data) narratives to those of policy narratives concerning migration. Rather than attempting to construct its own narrative of migration, the work examines the limits on which migration is creatively imagined within the scope of currently available narratives, specifically attempting to highlight the distinctions between those narratives.

To that end, the study addresses the following research questions concerning migration from the NT:

RQ1. How do causal claims made about migration differ between news media, stakeholder, and policy narratives? (how do sense-making claims vary)

RQ2. How do exclusion–inclusion claims about migration and migrants differ between news media, stakeholder, and policy narratives? (how is self distinguished from other from each vantage point)

RQ3. How do phenomena of interests concerning migration differ between news media, stakeholder, and policy narratives? (how are narratives structured around principle acts, agents, scenes, instruments, purposes)

RQ4. What are the constraints and overlays of possible imagined outcomes associated with migration shared and contested between news media, stakeholder, and policy narratives?

REFERENCES

Aalberg, T., & Beyer, A. (2015). Human interest framing of irregular immigration: An empirical study of public preferences for personalized news stories in the United States, France, and Norway. *American Behavioral Scientist, 59*(7), 858–875. https://doi.org/10.1177/00027642155732

Akesson, L., & Baaz, M. E. (Eds.) (2015). *Africa's return migrants: The new developers?* Zed Books. https://doi.org/10.5040/9781350218239

Alba, Francisco. "1. Evolving Migration Responses in Mexico and the United States: Diverging Paths?". *Mexican Migration to the United States: Perspectives From Both Sides of the Border*, edited by Harriett D. Romo and Olivia Mogollon-Lopez, New York, USA: University of Texas Press, 2016, pp. 17-36. https://doi.org/10.7560/308974-004

Bauder, H. (2018). Westphalia, migration, and feudal privilege. *Migration Letters, 15*(3), 333–346. https://doi.org/10.59670/ml.v15i3.356

Bechara, A., Damasio H., & Damasio, A. R. (2000). Emotion, decision making and the orbitofrontal cortex. *Cerebral Cortex, 10*(3), 295–307. https://doi.org/10.1093/cercor/10.3.295

Beck, U. (1992). *Risk society: Towards a new modernity.* Sage.

Beck, U. (1998). Politics of risk society. In J. Franklin (Ed.), *The politics of risk society* (pp. 9–22). Polity.

Beckett, D., & Morris, G. (2001). Ontological performance: Bodies, identities and learning. *Studies in the Education of Adults*, *33*(1), 35–48.

Benson, R. (2013). *Shaping immigration news*. Cambridge University Press.

Benson, R., & Wood, T. (2015). Who says what or nothing at all? Speakers, frames, and frameless quotes in unauthorized immigration news in the United States, Norway, and France. *American Behavioral Scientist*, *59*(7), 802–821. https://doi.org/10.1177/0002764215573257

Blinder, S., & Allen, W. L. (2016). Constructing immigrants: Portrayals of migrant groups in British national newspapers, 2010–2012. *International Migration Review*, *50*(1), 3–40. https://doi.org/10.1111/imre.12206

Boswell, C., Geddes, A., & Scholten, P. (2011). The role of narratives in migration policy-making: A research framework. *The British Journal of Politics and International Relations*, *13*(1), 1–11. https://doi.org/10.1111/j.1467-856X.2010.00435.x

Busselle, R., & Bilandzic, H. (2008). Fictionality and perceived realism in experiencing stories: A model of narrative comprehension and engagement. *Communication Theory*, *18*(2), 255–280. https://doi.org/10.1111/j.1468-2885.2008.00322.x.

Cisneros, J. D. (2008). Contaminated communities: The metaphor of "immigrant as pollutant" in media representations of immigration. *Rhetoric and Public Affairs*, 11(4), 569–601. https://doi.org/10.1353/rap.0.0068

Collingwood, L., & O'Brien Gonzalez, B. (2019). Public opposition to sanctuary cities in Texas: Criminal threat or immigration threat?. *Social Science Quarterly*, *100*(4), 1182–1196. https://doi.org/10.1111/ssqu.12632

Cooley, S., Hinck, R., & Sample, E. (2022). Northern triangle and Mexican news media perspectives on the migration crisis: strategic narrative and the identification of good action. *Migration and Development*, *11*(3), 291-313.

Crow, D., & Jones, M. (2018). Narratives as tools for influencing policy change. *Policy & Politics*, *46*(2), 217–234. https://doi.org/10.1332/030557318X15230061022899

Crow, D. A., & Lawlor, A. (2016). Media in the policy process: Using framing and narratives to understand policy influences. *Review of Policy Research*, *33*(5), 472–491. https://doi.org/10.1111/ropr.12187

Czarniawska, B. (1998). *A narrative approach to organization studies*. Sage. https://doi.org/10.4135/9781412983235.

Daiute, C., & Nelson, K. (1997). Making sense of the sense-making. *Journal of Narrative and Life History*, *7*(1-4), 297–215, 209. https://doi.org/10.1075/jnlh.7.1-4.25mak

Dal Lago, A. (2009). *Non-Persons: the exclusion of migrants in a global society*. Ipoc Press.

Del Vicario, M., Scala, A., Caldarelli, G., Stanley, H. E., & Quattrociocchi W. (2017). Modeling confirmation bias and polarization. *Scientific Reports*, *7*(1), 1–9. https://doi.org/10.1038/srep40391

Dennison, J. (2019). A review of public issue salience: Concepts, determinants and effects on voting. *Political Studies Review*, *17*(4), 436–446. https://doi.org/10.1177/1478929918819264

Dennison, J. (2021). Narratives: A review of concepts, determinants, effects, and uses in migration research. *Comparative Migration Studies*, *9*(1), 1–14.

Dennison, J., & Geddes, A. (2019). A rising tide? The salience of immigration and the rise of anti-immigration political parties in Western Europe. *The Political Quarterly*, *90*(1), 107–116. https://doi.org/10.1111/1467-923X.12620

Esses, V. M., Medianu, S., & Lawson, A. S. (2013). Uncertainty, threat, and the role of the media in promoting the dehumanization of immigrants and refugees. *Journal of Social Issues*, *69*(3), 518–536. https://doi.org/10.1111/josi.12027

Estrada, E. P., Ebert, K., & Liao, W. (2020). Polarized toward apathy: An analysis of the privatized immigration-control debate in the Trump Era. *PS: Political Science & Politics*, *53*(4), 679–684.

Farris, E. M., & Silber Mohamed, H. (2018). Picturing immigration: how the media criminalizes immigrants. *Politics, Groups, and Identities*, *6*(4), 814–824. https://doi.org/10.1080/21565503.2018.1484375

Gabrielatos, C., & Baker, P. (2008). Fleeing, sneaking, flooding: A corpus analysis of discursive constructions of refugees and asylum seekers in the UK press, 1996-2005. *Journal of English linguistics*, *36*(1), 5–38. https://doi.org/10.1177/0075424207311247

Galef, J. (2010). Uncertainty in science. *The Humanist*, *70*(1), 10.

Galef, J. (2021). *The Scout Mindset: Why some people see things clearly and others don't*. Penguin.

Green, M. C., & Brock, T. C. (2002). In the mind's eye: Transportation-imagery model of narrative persuasion. In M. C. Green, J. Strange, & T. C. Brock (Eds.), *Narrative impact: Social and cognitive foundations* (pp. 315–341). Lawrence Erlbaum Associates Publishers.

Green, M. E. (2020). Political imaginary of a postcapitalist climate. *Rethinking Marxism*, *32*(4), 412–416. https://doi.org/10.1080/08935696.2020.1807182

Greussing, E., & Boomgaarden, H. G. (2017). Shifting the refugee narrative? An automated frame analysis of Europe's 2015 refugee crisis. *Journal of Ethnic and Migration Studies*, *43*(11), 1749–1774. https://doi.org/10.1080/13691 83X.2017.1282813

Hallin, D. C. (2015). The dynamics of immigration coverage in comparative perspective. *American Behavioral Scientist*, *59*(7), 876–885. https://doi .org/10.1177/0002764215573259

Harris, C. T., & Gruenewald, J. (2020). News media trends in the framing of immigration and crime, 1990–2013. *Social Problems*, *67*(3), 452–470. https:// doi.org/10.1093/socpro/spz024

Hinck, R., Cooley, A., Cooley, S. C., & Kitsch, S. (2021). *The future of global competition: Ontological security and narratives in Chinese, Iranian, Russian, and Venezuelan media*. Routledge.

Hitchcock, W. I. (2023). CHAPTER 26."SHITHOLE COUNTRIES" Was Trump's Foreign Policy Racist?. In *Chaos Reconsidered: The Liberal Order and the Future of International Politics* (pp. 291-303). Columbia University Press.

Hoffman, D. D., & Prakash, C. (2014). Objects of consciousness. *Frontiers in Psychology*, *5*, 577. https://doi.org/10.3389/fpsyg.2014.00577

Horsti, K. (2008). Hope and despair: Representations of Europe and Africa in Finnish news coverage of "migration crisis." *Estudos em Comunicacao*, *3*, 125–155.

Hyde, S. D. (2020). Democracy's backsliding in the international environment. *Science*, *369*(6508), 1192–1196. https://doi.org/10.1126/science.abb2434

Innes, A. J. (2010). When the threatened become the threat: The construction of asylum seekers in British media narratives. *International Relations*, *24*(4), 456–477. https://doi.org/10.1177/0047117810385882

Jones, M. D. (2010). *Heroes and villains: Cultural narratives, mass opinions, and climate change*. The University of Oklahoma.

Jones, M. D., & McBeth, M. K. (2020). Narrative in the Time of Trump: Is the narrative policy framework good enough to be relevant? *Administrative Theory & Praxis*, *42*(2), 91–110. https://doi.org/10.1080 /10841806.2020.1750211

Killingsworth, M. A., & Gilbert, D. T. (2010). A wandering mind is an unhappy mind. *Science*, *330*(6006). https://doi.org/10.1126/science.1192439.

Krebs, R. (2015). *Narrative and the making of US national security*. Cambridge University Press.

Kuhn, T. S. (2012). *The structure of scientific revolutions*. University of Chicago press.

Lawlor, A., & Crow, D. (2018). Risk-based policy narratives. *Policy Studies Journal*, *46*(4), 843–867. https://doi.org/10.1111/psj.12270

Lee, E. J., & Shin, S. Y. (2014). When the medium is the message: How transportability moderates the effects of politicians' twitter communication. *Communication Research*, *41*(8), 1088–1110. https://doi .org/10.1177/0093650212466407

Lodge, M., & Taber, C. S. (2005). The automaticity of affect for political leaders, groups, and issues: An experimental test of the hot cognition hypothesis. *Political Psychology*, *26*(3), 455–482. https://doi .org/10.1111/j.1467-9221.2005.00426.x.

Mamadouh, V. (2012). The scaling of the 'invasion': A geopolitics of immigration narratives in France and the Netherlands. *Geopolitics*, *17*(2), 377–401. https://doi.org/10.1080/14650045.2011.578268.

McBeth, M. K., Jones, M. D., & Shanahan, E. A. (2014). The narrative policy framework. *Theories of the Policy Process*, *3*, 225–266.

Mitzen, J. (2006). Ontological security in world politics: State identity and the security dilemma. *European Journal of International Relations*, *12*(3), 341–370. https://doi.org/10.1177/1354066106067346

Mousin, C. B. (2019). Rights disappear when US policy engages children as weapons of deterrence. *AMA Journal of Ethics*, *21*(1), E58–E66. https://doi .org/10.1001/amajethics.2019.58

Oatley, K. (1995). A taxonomy of the emotions of literary response and a theory of identification in fictional narrative. *Poetics*, *23*(1-2), 53–74. https:// doi.org/10.1016/0304-422X(94)P4296-S

Palau-Sampio, D. (2019). Reframing Central American migration from narrative journalism. *Journal of Communication Inquiry, 43*(1), 93–114. https://doi.org/10.1177/0196859918806676

Pécoud, A. (2015). *Depoliticising migration: Global governance and international migration narratives.* Palgrave Macmillan.

Polansky, S., & Rieger, T. (2020). *Cognitive biases: Causes, effects, and implications for effective messaging-quick look.* NSI Inc Boston United States.

Prince, G. (1982). *Narratology.* Mouton.

Ricoeur, P. (1980). Narrative Time. *Critical Inquiry, 7*(1), 169–190. https://doi.org/10.1086/448093.

Ricoeur, P. (1984). *Time and narrative, Volume I.* The University of Chicago Press.

Roe, E. (1994). *Narrative policy analysis: Theory and practice.* Duke University Press.

Sconfienza, U. (2017). *The politics of environmental narratives.* Tilburg University.

Shanahan, E. A., Jones, M. D., & McBeth, M. K. (2011). Policy narratives and policy processes. *Policy Studies Journal, 39*(3), 535–561. https://doi.org/10.1111/j.1541-0072.2011.00420.x.

Shenhav, S. R. (2005). Concise narratives: A structural analysis of political discourse. *Discourse Studies, 7*(3), 315–335. https://doi.org/10.1177/1461445605052189.

Shenhav, S. R. (2006). Political narratives and political reality. *International Political Science Review, 27*(3), 245–262. https://doi.org/10.1177/0192512106064474.

Slaven, M., & Boswell, C. (2019). Why symbolise control? Irregular migration to the UK and symbolic policy-making in the 1960s. *Journal of Ethnic and Migration Studies, 45*(9), 1477–1495. https://doi.org/10.1080/1369183X.2018.1459522

Steinhilper, E., & Gruijters, R. J. (2018). A contested crisis: Policy narratives and empirical evidence on border deaths in the Mediterranean. *Sociology, 52*(3), 515–533. https://doi.org/10.1177/0038038518759248

Stenis, J. (2020). An economic instrument to improve migration. *Applied Economics and Finance, 7*(1), 15–20. https://doi.org/10.11114/aef.v7i1.4630

Stewart, J. (2012). Fiction over facts: How competing narrative forms explain policy in a new immigration destination. *Sociological Forum, 27*(3), 591–616. https://doi.org/10.1111/j.1573-7861.2012.01337.x.

Suro, R. (2008). *The triumph of no: How the media influence the immigration debate.* Brookings Institution. https://www.brookings.edu/wp-content/uploads/2012/04/0925_immigration_dionne.pdf

Swanson, L. R. (2016). The predicitive processing paradigm has roots in Kant. *Frontiers in Systems Neuroscience, 10*, 79. https://doi.org/10.3389/fnsys.2016.00079

Sytas, A., & Plucinska, J. (2021). Neighbours of Belarus say migrant crisis risks military clash. *Europe. Reuters*, November 11, 2021.

Thorbjørnsrud, K. (2015). Framing Irregular Immigration in Western Media. *American Behavioral Scientist, 59*(7), 771–782. https://doi.org/10.1177/0002764215573255

Waldorf, B. (2018). A network-based model of international migration. In *Crossing borders* (pp. 339–352). Routledge.

Wilson, G. M. (2005). Narratives. In J. Levinson (Ed.), *The Oxford handbook of aesthetics.* (pp.392-407). Oxford University Press

CHAPTER 2

Methods

The project attempted to answer research questions by deploying a mixed methods design, triangulating data across three different methodologies: qualitative analysis of migration policy briefings, in-depth interviews with migration policy stakeholders, and AI-human-in-the-loop quantitative analysis of news media coverage of migration from US, Mexican, Salvadoran, Honduran, and Guatemalan sources.

This chapter elaborates on the methodological design, first, by discussing the process of selection, recruitment and conducting of interviews with relevant stakeholders; second, by justifying the decision for examining news media articles on the topic and providing details on the content analysis protocols; and, third, by reviewing the selection and qualitative coding of relevant policy briefs. The chapter concludes with the justification for the triangulation of narratives across interview and news media data, with a special emphasis on sense-making from narrative analysis.

Stakeholder Interviews

Our project team reached out to over 200 migration-related stakeholders as well as members of the migrant community who had entered the US without legal status.[1] A stakeholder is broadly defined by *Merriam-Webster* as "one who is involved in or affected by a course of action"[2] and by the American Society for Quality as any "individual or group that has an interest in any decision or

---

[1] Of note, the initial study design included site visits to Mexico and border communities in the US; due to COVID-19 restrictions on travel and accessibility, the project pivoted to internet-based interviews in substitution.

[2] https://www.merriam-webster.com/dictionary/stakeholder

activity of an organization."[3] Here, migration policy stakeholders were identified as those individuals whose occupation, volunteer function, expertise, and/or
life experience made the subject of US migration policy and/or migration coming from the Northern Triangle a key interest with which they could discuss
their insights. Numerous snowball samples were conducted across a variety
of experts as individuals responded to initial outreach efforts. The purpose of
the stakeholder interviews was to provide individual vantages on narrative
sense-making, inclusion–exclusion criteria claims, phenomena of interest, and
imagined outcomes.

Researchers generated a list of possible participants by canvassing migration policy centers across the globe; migrant shelters in the US, Mexico, and
Northern Triangle; migration vocational training centers; journalists and filmmakers covering migration; academics with migration and/or Central American
specializations; faith-based organizations with relief efforts in the Northern
Triangle; immigration lawyers in the US specializing in asylum cases; law enforcement from the US and Mexico; as well as reaching out to migrant communities in the US.

Respondents to initial outreach efforts were sent electronic copies of the
OSU-IRB–approved oral informed consent, as well as a list of questions to
guide the interview. Interview participants agreed to take part in the study on
the condition of confidentiality given the sensitive nature of some of the discussions. Interviews were led by a specialist in in-depth interview methodology
and were semi-structured in nature.

Researchers asked interviewees a series of open-ended questions to allow
the interviewee to give their perspectives in a detailed manner. Questions were
formatted to allow the interviewee be guided within a structure, while not influencing their answer. This was chosen due to the expected variety of answers
based on the complexity of the issue, as well as the varied backgrounds and
specialties of those interviewed. Questions asked included perspectives on the
primary causes of immigration, practical fixes (if unconstrained by budgets
and resources), the role the US could potentially play in the region going forward, as well as questions pertaining to each interviewee's area of specialty.
Interviews were conducted in the native language of the interviewee, either in
English or in Spanish.

All interview recordings were stored on a password-protected cloud service, as well as a password-protected portable hard drive. Transcriptions of the

---

[3] https://asq.org/quality-resources/stakeholders

recorded interviews were completed in order to remove all identifying information from the data analyzed. Following the interview, participants were asked for a list of other potential interview candidates within their network and were offered the opportunity to review the final project report prior to its dissemination to Department of Homeland Security (DHS), as an integrity check ensuring confidentiality and accuracy.

A total of forty migration stakeholders were interviewed for this project. These included renowned migration policy experts and academics; award-winning migration documentary filmmakers; internationally recognized journalists; migrant shelter workers and relief/development volunteers working in the US, El Salvador, Guatemala, and Mexico; migrant vocational trainers and re-settlement officers; immigration lawyers, US border law enforcement and DHS personnel; and migrants who entered the US without legal status. Interview transcripts were inductively assessed for codes and themes using a grounded theory approach.

Themes and codes were then organized and summarized around the four primary research questions of the study, with particular attention given to the narrative structure (act, agent, scene, instrument, purpose) of each interview. Table 2.1 lists a breakdown of interview participants by stakeholder classification.

Table 2.1: Interview Participants by Stakeholder Classification

Stakeholder category	Examples of stakeholders	Number of interviewees
Policy experts	Renowned migration policy experts; IGO migration expert; NGO migration expert; immigration lawyers; resettlement officers	13
Shelter workers	Migrant shelter workers; relief/development volunteers; missionaries; shelter volunteers	10
Academics	Policy professors; director of academic center; migration researchers	6
Vocational trainers	Migrant vocational trainers	3
Migrants	Migrants who entered the US without documentation	3

(Continued)

Stakeholder category	Examples of stakeholders	Number of interviewees
Journalists	Award-winning migration documen-tary filmmaker; NT journalists	3
Law enforcement	US border law enforcement officer; DHS officer	2

News Media Coverage

Data analyzed from the media component included news articles from Mexico, US, and NT sources spanning the period January 1999 to December 2019. The purpose of the news media data was to provide cultural vantages, particularly at the nation-state level, on narrative sense-making, inclusion–exclusion criteria claims, phenomena of interest, and imagined outcomes. Further, in order to determine how narratives on migration have shifted over time, the data was split into four time periods based on major legislative debates over US immigration reform:

Time Period 1: One year before and after Congress's passing of the 2000 Legal Immigration Family Equity Act.

Time Period 2: The 2005 to 2007 US House and Senate debates on immigration.

Time Period 3: One year before and after the 2012 Deferred Action for Childhood Arrivals (DACA) and 2013 Gang of Eight debates.

Time Period 4: Coverage from 2015 to 2019.

Data was primarily collected utilizing the Dow Jones Factiva international news archive made available by Oklahoma State University. Additional archives, including Gale World Scholar as well as individual online newspapers, were used to collect Mexican news reports from Time Period 1 and Northern Triangle countries from Time Periods 2, 3, and 4. Search terms used to collect news articles for analysis included immigrant/immigration and migrant/migration, translated into both English and Spanish.

For the US sources, articles were collected from the *New York Times*, *Washington Post*, and *Wall Street Journal*. Mexican sources included *El Norte*, *Word*, *Reforma*, *Mura*, *El Universal*, *El Financiero*, and *La Journada*. NT sources included *La Tribuna*, *Presna Libre*, *El Diario de Hoy*, *El Siglo*, *Diario co Latino*, *Diario de Centro América*, and *El Nuevo Dia*. Articles were systematically random sampled at over a 99% CI (confidence interval). In total, 53,441 articles were collected: 17,772 from Mexico, 27,600 from the US, and 8,069 from NT (See Table 2.2).

Data Analysis

To identify the narratives reported in the US, Mexico, and NT news media on migration, researchers employed multiple AI human-in-the-loop methodologies.

First, to identify the overarching narrative structures present in the reporting, researchers trained their own supervised machine learning algorithm to identify issues related to region of migrant origin, responsibility for managing migration, voices reported, argument type, migrant emotions, perceptions of migrants, reasons for migration, discussion of migrant journey and immigration policies.

Table 2.2: Articles Collected for Analysis

	US	Mexico	NT	Total
Time Period 1	2,900	1,514	NA	4,414
Time Period 2	6,600	4,400	397	11,397
Time Period 3	5,100	3,058	1,707	9,865
Time Period 4	13,000	8,800	5,965	27,765
Total	27,600	17,772	8,069	53,441

Second, researchers identified individual narrative themes by using topic clustering algorithms comparing news content by region and time period. Six clusters for each country's reporting during the time period were produced with human analysis summarizing exemplar articles from each cluster. To further validate the narrative themes present, researchers also categorized the top 75 parts of speech (POS) in conjunction with keyword-in-context (KWIC) from each country's reporting during the four time periods around words correlating with "migrant" and "migration." These terms were then grouped by the five elements of a narrative, including acts, agents, scene, instruments, and purpose/ motive. The KWIC analysis provided contextual depictions of how these terms were discussed, allowing for identification of additional key narrative elements.

Finally, researchers identified a list of key terms for valence analysis to determine the emotional nature of their usage. A valence algorithm trained on Twitter data identified average valence scores of sentences mentioning each term.

AI Algorithms

Relevant news articles were manually extracted into files containing the news articles and separated into folders based on region and time period. Individual articles were recovered using heuristic splitting rules determined from the data, and duplicate articles were culled by computing a Jaccard similarity score between each article and previous articles, dropping those with a score greater than 0.8. US articles were filtered to only those that contained mentions of any of the following: Mexico, Northern Triangle, Honduras, El Salvador, Guatemala, Central America, or Latin America.

Because articles can vary in length and may discuss several topics, each article was split into non-overlapping windows containing five sentences (smaller windows sometimes appear due to sentences at the end of each article). These windows were then filtered to those that contained "migrant," "immigrant," or variants of the two words.

Sentiment Analysis

Sentiment analysis was performed using the VADER (Valence-Aware Dictionary for Sentiment Reasoning) model (Hutto & Gilbert, 2014). VADER uses both a lexicon of words with associated valence scores and a set of rules for modifying valence scores, including capitalization, punctuation, and modifier words. Although VADER is tuned for analysis of social media, the original article shows that the algorithm generalizes to other contexts. After scoring each five-sentence window, researchers analyzed the mean scores of windows containing various terms/phrases.

Clustering

After splitting into windows, common words were removed to identify the unique terms associated with each cluster. For this, we used a set of common English words, a collection of words that often appear in news media,[4] and a small set of custom words based on manual inspection of the data. All remaining words in each window were stemmed using standard tools from the NLTK library (Bird et al., 2009), reducing words to their word stem, base or root form.

To facilitate insight discovery at multiple levels of granularity, several groups of windows were analyzed: all windows together, windows from each region (separately), windows from each time period (separately), and windows from each pair of region and time period. Since there were three regions and four time periods, in total there were 20 analysis groups.

To produce numeric vectors that can be used by clustering algorithms, the windows were vectorized by computing tf-idf (Spärck Jones, 2004) scores for the 1,000 most frequent words and two-word phrases. These scores depend both on the number of times a term appears in a window and on the number of windows in which it appears and are normalized to avoid long windows from producing excessive scores.

Once vectorized, the data was clustered using the KMeans method (MacQueen, 1967). The number of clusters used differed based on the windows considered: the analysis group with all windows was partitioned into 20 clusters, all windows in a given region or time period were partitioned into 12 clusters, and all windows in a given region/time period pair were partitioned into six clusters. For each cluster, we computed the ten closest windows to each cluster centroid and the 20 words with the highest tf-idf score for the cluster's centroid. The latter was also used to describe each analysis group, averaging over all windows in each group.

To visualize the data, the tf-idf scores were projected into two dimensions using principal component analysis (Pearson, 1901). The scikit-learn (Pedregosa et al., 2011) Python library was used for vectorizing, clustering, and visualization.

Classification

For classification, five sentence windows were labeled by a human coder for each of the 20 classification problems. The data was preprocessed in a manner

---

[4.] Derived from "A huge list of stopwords collected from millions of news articles" https://github.com/vikasing /news-stopwords

similar to the clustering task, with minor differences. Tf-idf scores were again used, keeping only the 300 most important terms.

A grid search was performed to select the best of several machine learning models and their associated hyperparameters, using three-fold cross validation to ensure statistical validity. We considered k-nearest neighbors, small neural networks, several support vector machine algorithms, and several random forest ensemble algorithms. The grid search also tuned a few parameters related to vectorization of the text. The mean cross-validated balanced accuracy ranged from a high of 73.5% (the "economy" category) to a low of 20.3% for the problem of determining whose ideas/experiences were being presented. We note that this last classification problem has eight classes, so any accuracy above 12.5% is better than chance.

Policy Briefs

The purpose of the policy briefing was to provide macro-system vantages on narrative sense-making, inclusion–exclusion criteria claims, phenomena of interest, and imagined outcomes. First, researchers conducted systematic qualitative assessments of migration policy literature. The review of policy briefs took an inductive and interpretive approach. Using qualitative content analysis, researchers systematically analyzed policy briefs, reports, and policy essays published on the subject of migration within the last five years (publication dates 2015–2020). The policy briefs were identified through an open source search using relevant keywords and snowball sampling. A total of fifty-seven policy briefs from 20 organizations are included within this study. Table 2.3 lists all organizations included in the policy documents review. The review took the Immigration Policies in Comparison (IMPIC) typology as a base toward further investigating labor migration policies, refugees/asylum seeker policies, and return/reintegration policies. This was chosen because these policy fields are the most widely discussed within the materials. The policy briefing review was guided by the following considerations: best examples of migration policy practices, suggested improvements to existing migration policies, and lessons learned from various migration policy postassessments.

Table 2.3: Organizations included In the Policy Documents Review

Abbreviation	Name	Website
WOLA	Washington Office on Latin America	www.wola.org
	Bipartisan Policy Center	www.bipartisan-policy.org
CGD	Center for Global Development	www.cgdev.org
CSIS	Center for Strategic and International Studies	www.csis.org
CFR	Council on Foreign Relations	www.cfr.org
	Creative Associates International	www.creativeas-sociatesinterna-tional.com
GFMD	Global Forum on Migration and Development	www.gfmd.org
KNOMAD	Global Knowledge Partnership on Migration and Development	www.www.kno-mad.org
ICMPD	International Centre for Migration Policy Development	www.icmpd.org
IOM	International Organization for Migration	www.iom.int
	Justice in Mexico	www.justicein-mexico.org
MEDAM	Mercator Dialogue on Asylum and Migration	www.medam-migration.eu
MPC	Migration Policy Center	www.migra-tionpolicycentre.eu
MPI	Migration Policy Institute	www.migra-tionpolicy.org

(*Continued*)

Abbreviation	*Name*	*Website*
	OECD Migration Policy Debates	www.oecd.org /migration
FMUMP	The Forced Migration Upward Mobility Project	www.fmump.org
TCM	Transatlantic Council on Migration	www.migra-tionpolicy.org
UNHCR	United Nations High Commissioner for Refugees	www.unhcr.org
WZB	World Bank Group	www.worldbank.org
	WZB Berlin Social Science Center	www.wzb.eu

Triangulating Narratives across Interview and News Media Data

Today's globalized world has brought individuals, civil society actors, and governments closer than ever before, resulting in a global networked society facilitated by communication (Castells, 2008, 2009). While mass media still plays an essential role in defining how communities understand their world, analysis of news reporting requires frameworks that capture multilevel environments among actors, news reports, and policy makers from the local to global and back (Gilboa et al., 2016). In recognizing the intrinsic difficulties Mexican and Central American news media experience when reporting on such a sensitive topic, this study adds in-depth interviews with migration experts and stakeholders.

Evaluating the systematic structure of individual and community narratives is an important factor in crafting intelligible policy. Crow and Lawlor (2016) argue that narrative frameworks impact policy discussions in that "narratives used by media, stakeholders, and citizens [are used] to describe policies, problems, and opponents [that] can be powerful in the context of shaping public opinion and policy agendas" (Crow & Lawlor, 2016, p. 475). Thus, narrative policy frameworks "[attempt] to integrate narratives as a series of empirically identifiable and measurable variables in a more clearly articulated manner" (Crow & Lawlor, 2016, p. 475). While simple, powerful messages influence public opinion on global policy issues, they can also undermine cooperative goals by minimizing the space for dialogue among stakeholders. Instead, focusing on the discursive elements of policy discussions by identifying, analyzing, and synthesizing publics' construction of persuasive arguments and counter-arguments from multiple stakeholders provides feedback for organizations to reflexively understand how their actions are understood, leading to the constitution of communities with shared meaning (Proedrou & Frangonikolopoulos, 2012).

In addition to taking societal level views on migration, taking an individual perspective places emphasis on personal narrative, including interpretations of the events unfolding before them. Thus, interviewing migrants about their journey opens up the narrative and reflects how that event happened in their own life (Fedyuk & Zentai, 2018). Additionally, interviewing individuals who work in the field—policy experts, shelter workers, law enforcement—provides their experience working with both the migrants and the policies surrounding the system. These individuals see both sides of the coin. Meanwhile, journalist and academic perspectives provide more commentary and comparison; they provide written accounts of events they hear, witness, or research that shines light on the situations that occur for these migrants.

Narrative analysis, however, goes beyond just analyzing discourse by including a strategic component: allowing actors greater influence in reaching their goals. As Roselle et al. (2014) argues, "strategic narrative *is* soft power in the 21st century" (Roselle et al., 2014, p. 71) and claims that narratives explain the world and set constraints on the imaginable and actionable and shape perceived interests. States – with particular characteristics or identities – are actors within the international system as we understand it today. Narratives can be a powerful resource setting out what characterizes any state in the world or how the world works. (p. 76)

Thus, understanding the narrative landscape in relation to the problem of transnational migration allows officials to construct and project narratives capable of influencing their operating environment. The concept of strategy in the analysis of narrative in this study considers what actions are being imagined, promoted, and constrained on a given subject within and across various communities and levels of larger transnational society.

REFERENCES

Bird, S., Loper, E., & Klein, E. (2009). Natural language processing with python. *O'Reilly*. https://www.oreilly.com/library/view/natural-language-processing /9780596803346/

Castells, M. (2008). The new public sphere: Global civil Society, communication networks, and global governance. *Annals of the American*

Academy of Political and Social Science, *616*(1), 78–93. https://doi
.org/10.1177/0002716207311877

Castells, M. (2009). *Communication power*. Oxford University Press.

Crow, D. A., & Lawlor, A. (2016). Media in the policy process: Using framing and narratives to understand policy influences. *Review of Policy Research*, *33*(5), 472–491. https://doi.org/10.1111/ropr.12187

Fedyuk, O., & Zentai, V. (2018). The interview in migration studies: A step towards a dialogue and knowledge co-production? In R. Zapata-Barrero & E. Yalaz (Eds.), *Qualitative research in European migration studies* (pp. 171–188). Springer.

Gilboa, E., Jumbert, M. G., Miklian, J., & Robinson, P. (2016). Moving media and conflict studies beyond the CNN effect. *Review of International Studies*, *42*(4). https://doi.org/10.1017/S026021051600005X

Hutto, C., & Gilbert, E. (2014, May). Vader: A parsimonious rule-based model for sentiment analysis of social media text. In *Proceedings of the international AAAI conference on web and social media* (Vol. 8, No. 1, pp. 216-225).

MacQueen, J. (1967, June). Some methods for classification and analysis of multivariate observations. In *Proceedings of the fifth Berkeley symposium on mathematical statistics and probability* (Vol. 1, No. 14, pp. 281-297).

Pearson, K. (1901). On lines and planes of closest fit to systems of points in space. *The London, Edinburgh, and Dublin Philosophical Magazine and Journal of Science*, *2*(11), 559–572. https://doi
.org/10.1080/14786440109462720

Pedregosa, F., Varoquaux, G., Gramfort, A., Michel, V., Thirion, B., Grisel, O., Blondel, M., Prettenhofer, P., Weiss, R., Dubourg, V., Vanderplas, J., Passos, A., Cournapeau, D., Brucher, M., Perrot, M., & Duchesnay, E. (2011). Scikit-learn: Machine learning in python. *Journal of Machine Learning Research*, *12*, 2825–2830. www.jmlr.org/papers/volume12/pedregosa11a/pedregosa11a.pdf

Proedrou, F., & Frangonikolopoulos, C. (2012). Refocusing public diplomacy: The need for strategic discursive public diplomacy. *Diplomacy and Statecraft*, *23*(4), 728–745. https://doi.org/10.1080/09592296.2012.736339

Roselle, L., Miskimmon, A., & O'Loughlin, B. (2014). Strategic narrative: A new means to understand soft power. *Media, War and Conflict*, 7(1), 70–84. https://doi.org/10.1177/1750635213516696

Spärck Jones, K. (2004). A statistical interpretation of term specificity and its application in retrieval. *Journal of Documentation*, 60(5), 493–502. https://doi.org/10.1108/00220410410560573

## CHAPTER 3

In-Depth Interviews

The following chapter highlights the key narrative findings common across all interviews, with particular attention given to sense-making claims, exclusion–inclusion claims, and the primary phenomenon of interests when discussing migration.

In-depth interviewing is a commonly used qualitative research method across disciplines, particularly in education, health care, and the social sciences. The goal of in-depth interviewing is to explore the lived experiences, perspectives, and deeper meanings behind people's actions, decisions, and behaviors (McCormack, 2004; Witz et al., 2001). In contrast to structured interviews or surveys with pre-determined response categories, in-depth interviews allow respondents to describe phenomena in their own words, reveal connections, and share stories that surveys cannot capture (McCormack, 2004). As such, in-depth interviews are optimal for understanding subjective experiences, gaining insights into respondents' inner worlds, and elucidating the contexts that shape their lives (Witz et al., 2001).

A central principle guiding in-depth interview research is the primacy of direct, subjective knowledge of the respondent's experiences, states of mind, and consciousness (Witz et al., 2001). The investigator aims to immerse themselves in the respondent's perspectives by identifying with the micro-analytic nuances, rhythms, tones, and pauses within their speech (Witz et al., 2001). This close listening and attunement to subtle verbal and nonverbal details allows the interviewer to grasp unspoken dimensions of meaning. The investigator's emerging subjective understandings are continually verified against the data through ongoing cycles of interviewing, analysis, and interpretation.

Stories serve as a key source of meaning and insight within in-depth interviews (McCormack, 2004). Narrative processes within respondents' speech, such as theorizing, arguing, augmenting, and storytelling, provide clues into how they make sense of their lives. The investigator identifies, enriches, and connects stories to compose an interpretive narrative illuminating the respondent's experiences in context. This narrative approach retains the situational uniqueness of each respondent's account while highlighting its complexity and individuality. Sharing interpretive stories with respondents throughout the research process enables collaborative meaning-making and member-checking (McCormack, 2004).

A defining feature of in-depth interview research is that findings emerge through inductive processes of intuition, immersion, identification, and introspection (Witz et al., 2001). The investigator strives to grasp the essential nature of the phenomenon as subjectively felt and lived by each respondent. Discerning these essences requires suspending pre-existing theoretical assumptions to see afresh. Findings are generalized by identifying commonalities in the essences across cases. This inductive orientation aligns with naturalistic inquiry paradigms that uphold emergent, contextualized knowledge produced through researcher–participant collaboration and negotiation (McCormack, 2004).

As discussed in the methodology chapter, a total of forty migration stakeholders were interviewed from the following categories: policy experts (n = 13), shelter workers (n = 10), academics (n = 6), vocational trainers (n = 3), migrants (n = 3), journalists (n = 3), and law enforcement officers (n = 2). The results of the thematic analyses of the narratives within the interviews are presented later.

Themes within Sense-Making Claims

The stakeholder interviews describe the underlying causal structures of migration coming from the Northern Triangle (NT) as a complex storm of interwoven factors, across which violence is the most pressing and prominent theme. All of the stakeholder groups spoke about staggering levels of violence and extortion in the NT that mars civil society, disrupts livelihoods, and forces people into desperate decisions in order to protect themselves and their family.

Interviewees attributed violence to pervasive corruption, starting with socio-political elites and matriculating down to every level of society. Corrupt governance is said to perpetuate historically weak and compromised state institutions, rendering them incapable of stemming gang violence or addressing socio-economic inequalities. Corruption further contributes to already vast gaps in wealth inequality throughout the NT, fostering violent, transaction-oriented fiefdoms of coalesced power. As one interviewee noted, at the end of the day, *"it's all about the money."* Unrelenting, unrestrained contestation for control of economically profitable spaces breeds toxic violence. As a consequence, the foundational lack of safety, incessant extortion, woefully corrupt, and, resultantly, under-resourced state systems are largely credited by interviewees as driving migration.

This is not to detract from other important themes within stakeholder narratives on the causal drivers of migration but simply to call attention to the fact that interviewees view the other factors catalyzing migration as foundationally linked to economic-incentivized violence and corruption. Violent conditions exacerbate the other motivating factors, particularly pervasive gang violence that is ideologically structured around maximizing profit and control.

Thus, the economic push and pull factors catalyzing migration are discussed in relation to poverty and economic opportunity, respectively. Four notable thematic distinctions arise throughout interviewee narratives concerning economic catalysts for migration important to how migration is made sense of holistically:

- First, economic migration is initially an issue of internal displacement, as people move from rural areas to nearby urban areas in search of stability.
- Second, rural migration is said to be undergirded by a lack of land access for rural farmers. Export-oriented agriculture companies use economic leverage, political leverage, and outright force to prevent rural farmers from having enough land to sustain communities or increase economic capacities.
- Third, climate change exacerbates the aforementioned land access difficulties. Years of intense drought, coupled with unseasonably intense storms and flooding, make crop failure more likely, as well as more devastating.
- Fourth, rural migrants are often indigenous peoples who speak native dialects as their primary, and sometimes only, language. Indigenous migrants face cultural and linguistic discriminatory barriers in the NT, becoming easy targets for exploitation as they move into urban areas.

The business of human trafficking is said to rival, and in some cases exceed, drug trafficking profitability for cartels, the implications of which further catalyze migration. Human smugglers take advantage of poorly understood, frequently changing, US immigration and asylum policies, advancing *"now or never"* arguments to would-be migrants in order to incentivize attempts to enter the US and justify prices. Migrants who are deported back to their country of origin often find themselves in cyclical debt traps to smugglers and cartels, forcing them to continually re-attempt entry to the US. Further, the tremendous backlog of cases in US immigration court system incentivizes attempts at illegal entry, as asylum backlogs make asylee claims unlikely to be heard in a reasonable time frame, while deportation backlogs make illegal entry more appealing. The ambiguity surrounding US immigration policies, associated costs and backlog of legal entry, and ability to stay in the US without documentation aid human smugglers in incentivizing illegal entry.

Technological and global social media connectivity is discussed as a key influencer of migration, as is the relative ease with which people can travel vast distances using modern transit. In particular, family connections in the US and remittances sent home demonstrate lifestyle disparities and possible opportunities for prosperity that embed migration as a known, and considered, option. The US is romanticized as a destination; as a consequence, migrants are often woefully uninformed of the migration process and not fully aware of all of the potential risks. Although the physical dangers of the migratory route are relatively well known in the NT, the combination of push factors (i.e., crippling violence, poverty, crime) and pull factors (i.e., access to land, search for safety, economic opportunities) overwhelm alternatives of staying for many.

Finally, many of the stakeholder groups noted that migration is a naturally occurring, historical, human phenomenon, impossible to genuinely contain, although possible to intelligently direct and steer toward developmental goals. The confluence of historical, climatic, institutional, economic, and criminal factors driving migration from the NT, all underpinned by catastrophic violence, have altered the demographics of migrants entering the US. Stakeholders noted that while young, opportunistic males seeking labor continue to come to the US, women and families fleeing violence now comprise the majority of migrants attempting to enter the US. This shift in demographics from individuals to family units blurs the ability to distinguish economic and safety-seeking migration.

Stakeholders most frequently discussed intolerable violence; systemic corruption; institutional failure; vast wealth inequality; US immigration court case backlogs; lack of rural land access; and the innate human tendency to seek safety, stability, and prosperity as the main causal factors of migration from the NT.

Expanded Sense-Making Findings

Here, the sense-making claims made by stakeholders are categorized relative to the vantage points offered, allowing the reader to see how each group of stakeholders differs in focus.

Migrant Sense-Making Claims

Migrants discuss the causes of migration through several push factors (poverty, crime, violence) and pull factors (search for safety, economic opportunities, and access to land). Notably, migrants distinguish gender differences in relation to the factors motivating migration; men are described as more likely to be in pursuit of economic opportunity and women as more likely to be directly fleeing violence. As one migrant notes, *"Women [are] more concerned with violence and protecting their children. Men [are] more concerned with economic opportunity."* Another migrant shared that his *"mother told him to get a better and safer job in the US due to rising gang violence."*

Crime and violence are cited most often as the underlying cause of migration. Respondents often talk about increasing levels of violence, suffering, and exploitation in their home countries, forcing people to flee. One respondent noted, *"Promises of wealth in the US are not a reality, but the safety is. Hard work, but worth it."*

Economics are often discussed as both a pull and push factor. One migrant reported that his migration journey was *"spurred on by lack of land access"* and that he migrated to the US to *"earn money to purchase land."* He further acknowledges that his *"migration [was] spurred by a want to escape poverty"* and that the risks were *"not fully considered in the moment."* Another migrant shared that the Bracero program[1] *"gave many Mexicans a taste of life in the US"* and that rural US destinations appeal to undocumented migrants because of lower costs of living and well-paying manual labor jobs.

Policy experts' Sense-Making Claims

Policy experts often discuss migration as a historic human process; *"migratory movements of people [are] natural ... [migration] cannot really be controlled."* However, they attribute the most recent upward trends in migration globally to technology developments, mobility increases, global violence, climate change, and vast resource inequalities. Policy experts also note a recent shift in migrant demographics, with an increased number of families fleeing instability rather than individual labor/opportunity seekers. This increase in familial migration creates difficulties in distinguishing between violence or economic motivated migration.

[1.] The Bracero program started in 1942 and allowed Mexican workers opportunities at the US farms, providing them with minimum wages, adequate living conditions, protections from forced military service, and guaranteed deposits into saving accounts in Mexico.

Policy experts view the history of violence in the region as a leading cause of the failed socio-governmental infrastructure contributing to mass migration. A large socio-economic gap compounded by a lack of resources, gang violence, and corruption have forced individuals in the NT to face two dangerous realities: stay at home or pack up and attempt migration. Staying where they are leaves them pervious to violence because elites and criminal organizations are above the law due to a weak criminal justice system. As one respondent said,

> *"Staying home can be more dangerous than attempting migration because of gang violence."*

Another elaborated:

> *"All three countries, particularly El Salvador and Honduras at the time, had extreme levels of homicides; people felt insecure in their communities, but also felt that the government was either unable or unwilling to protect them."*

Violence is frequently cited as a cause of asylum claims—claims that are often rejected because of migrants' inability to obtain legal assistance, language resources, or financial resources required to go through the entire asylum process. Asylum seekers are described as simply being glad to get out of the line of fire. As one policy expert describes it, *"Being here in the US, even in detention or waiting a long time for process, or even being separated from family members, it is worth it to them to stay alive."*

Notably, migration is described as a profitable business for smugglers, local corrupt authorities, and gangs. As smugglers *"prey on migrants in countries of origin, corrupt authorities prey on them in transit nations."* Migrants are in *"desperate situations in their own countries,"* and they *"put themselves into debt and risk a violent journey to sometimes be deported, where criminal organizations take advantage yet again."* This creates a vicious cycle in which migrants get caught in debt traps that force them to continue attempts at reentry.

Climate change is often discussed as an underlying catalyst to migration. A lack of income and general food insecurity due to years of drought, crop failure, and torrential storm systems drive rural and indigenous populations first to local cities, where they often experience exploitation that drives their migration. As farmers leave the countryside, money is not cycled back into rural economies, which is necessary for other services to be available, further impoverishing the area. Finally, such exodus takes skills, experience, and cultural knowledge out of rural communities, demoralizing areas.

Academic Sense-Making Claims

When discussing causes of migration, academics distinguish between push and pull factors, focusing more on the first category. Among push factors, the following picture emerges: economic conditions, corruption, inequality, and violence all contribute to migrants leaving their homes.

Violence is one of the most frequently discussed push factors, for the threat of life and livelihood is a real concern. As one academic put it, "*The sort of violence that we're seeing in the region having to do with criminal violence and other forms of violence that are the drivers of the current migration crisis and are issues that were never truly addressed.*" Violence is often described as systematic, extremely organized, and unprecedented: "*Violence that I saw in my time in El Salvador eclipses what most see in their entire lives.*" People are forced to pay *impuesto de guerra*—the war tax—and are often caught as collateral damage between opposing gangs. Violence toward women and indigenous people are of particular note. One academic describes the situation in detail:

> *In Mexico, the women would gather on this bus to go to this factory outside of town, never seen again. Because they said what happens is guys chase them and gang rape and kill them. Very rotten, in the desert. It happens all the time.*

Another offers his perspective on violence toward indigenous people: "*One can be killed for being indigenous; persecuted for advocating for environmental rights.*"

Violence is closely associated with the economic push factors, for "*violence is used to extract resources from the economy, and to become a power player.*" When discussing economic push factors, interviewees generally reference competition for scarce resources in the region and share perspectives on two-step migration patterns. First, people migrate from rural regions to urban areas because of displacement from land (internal migration). Then, they embark on longer migration journeys to the North (external migration). Violence is also closely related to corruption. As one academic describes it,

> *And so it's more about the violence and the corruption and the sort of lack of overall governance, domestic violence of all kinds, etc. That is really pushing people to leave. I don't think that many governments in the region think that immigration is necessarily a bad thing because it releases pressure.*

In many instances, Central American governments put considerations of power before considerations of compassion, contributing to "*endemic and expected corruption.*" Academics are also keen to point out that recent efforts to combat corruption (such as UN-sponsored Commission against Impunity in Guatemala [CICIG]) have been undermined by the Trump administration.

Structural inequality is a commonly discussed push factor. Specifically, the lack of access to land and farming is determined as a major cause of migration. For example, one interviewee said, "*Neoliberal economic policies that continue to kind of favor large multinational corporations instead of smaller peasant farmers have also exacerbated land inequality issues and have contributed then to more recent waves of migration.*"

Academics discuss the pull factors less often, although they consider them as being part of the same problems within the region. Economics is certainly a migration pull factor. In rural Guatemala, for example, it is "*rare to find a community that has not been touched by migration in some way,*" because many have moved North for better economic opportunities. One respondent elaborated: "*People are asking their relatives to build them these [big] homes that they'll have then to return to. And they're much bigger and much more modern than other homes.*" Safety is another important pull factor. As one academic describes it, migrants believe the US is…

> *a very safe place to live, a safe place to raise a family, a place where their children would be able to go to school, where there's services like that that their children can do despite being indigenous, for example, and you know a place where it's not necessarily free of racism, but where they're not daily living under a threat for their lives.*

Journalist Sense-Making Claims

When discussing causes of migration, journalists tended to report on migration in light of survival. Survival can be expanded into a multitude of factors, although it most commonly consisted of fleeing from violence, economic hardship, and food insecurities. Violence is cited as one of the key survival factors causing NT migration. Acts of violence ranged from extortion to harassment and forced recruitment. If migrants chose not to cooperate, the consequences tended to be severe. One journalist quotes a migrant who describes himself as *"running not because of the economy ... It was my son, I couldn't leave them there, I couldn't leave my daughter. I had no choice; I had to get out of there."*

Economic hardship and food insecurity are other motivations presented by journalists. Rural communities are particularly vulnerable to climate change–driven crop failures. As one respondent put it, *"Failure of the Guatemalan coffee harvest was the first wave of substantial climate migration that the US has seen."* Another interviewee elaborated:

> *People will do whatever is necessary to try to stay alive, keep their families healthy, fed and well. So, when you're not able to raise enough money to send your kids to school, you will migrate because you've seen others doing it and others benefiting.*

Among other factors is the belief that because many have gone through the process and finished the journey, one can do it, too. This belief is fueled by both personal accounts of family members and friends as well as disinformation supplanted by smugglers. Clearly one's social circle carries a great amount of weight: *"If my brother made it, I can make it..."* The situation is further compounded by a *"blind faith"* that is *"born of desperation in many instances and born of mind setting by people promoting their services as smugglers and people promoting welfare out of material goods."*

Shelter Worker Sense-Making Claims

When discussing causes of migration, shelter workers frequently discuss the change in migration demographics in the past two decades. Single men seeking jobs no longer constitute the primary migration group. Rather, there are more families seeking economic opportunity and refuge from violence. Many migrants leave development programs because they are still willing to do what is necessary to get to the US, and one respondent estimated that up to 80% of migrants mark the US as their final destination. According to shelter workers, migrants also pursue illegal crossings because they are denied viable paths of legal entrance.

Rural living conditions are cited as potential causes of migration problems. Shelter workers link rural living conditions to extremely poor health care, dental care, and diets, and limited access to clean water. One respondent describes rural NT houses as "*adobe straw homes with corrugated tin roofs that are not sealed all the way around ... dirt floors, for the most part.*" Furthermore, men in rural areas frequently abuse and abandon their families, leaving their children vulnerable to gang culture.

Shelter workers maintain that the US has frequently intervened in NT politics since the Cold War and that it has consistently refused to acknowledge that it has contributed, at least in part, to the instability of the region. As one respondent put it, "*The US needs to recognize that it did play a role in leading the Northern Triangle to its current circumstances.*" Respondents also highlight that the US has continually come in with solutions that address only one aspect of the issue and often succeeds in merely crippling the local economy.

Law Enforcement Sense-Making Claims

Law enforcement participants discuss two causes of migration: violence and ineffective US policies. The US is viewed as an intervening state in matters of other countries, which contributes to "*economic instability ... and other issues that in turn can cripple that economy.*" A more holistic plan to managing migration is clearly preferable to the law enforcement personnel. The second identified cause of migration is violence in the region, with highly powerful and ruthless cartels and gangs being responsible. As one participant commented:

> The most common issue I saw was just extreme violence where they were. A lot of them ... are families with young kids whose parents just really wanted to give them the ability to grow up and not be forced into gangs. A really common story I heard was families that had been targeted by cartels or gangs that had wanted their younger sons to work for them, and when the families would resist, their homes would be burned down, their sons would be forcibly taken or their daughters would be kidnapped in order to get to the son. And at that point, they felt like they didn't have a choice.

Vocational Trainer Sense-Making Claims

Vocational trainers did not discuss causes of migration in their interviews.

Themes within Exclusion–Inclusion Claims

Exclusion–inclusion claims centered primarily on discussion of the US asylum process, border policies, and the detrimental politicization of migration, particularly during the Trump administration. The US asylum process is seen as outdated and ill-suited to handling the influx of migrants seeking to establish residency on the basis of being a failing-state refugee. Language barriers from rural indigenous migrants who speak little or no Spanish creates further complications. Administrative processes are often unclear, and the system itself is described as backlogged and overloaded. Ultimately, the detention process is described as prison-like, with few chances of establishing the veracity of claims made. Legal entry into the US based on asylum-seeking status is described as a lengthy, expensive, and exhaustive process.

A broad scope of policies and restrictions made by the US to reduce legal entry are described as incentivizing illegal entry attempts and contributing to the criminal cartel control of human smuggling into the US. Rather than attempting the legal US entry process, migrants prefer to use human smugglers (coyotes) to navigate crossing expenses with criminal networks on their behalf in payments ranging from "*$2,000 to $12,000 per person*," depending on accommodations. The preparatory training for migrants crossing the border under the direction of criminal groups can take months and has become increasingly dangerous in recent years. Migrants are often given backpacks filled with a few provisions and left to navigate harsh ranchlands, some are left in *stash-houses* for months, some held for ransom, others indiscriminately pressed into dangerous services; many die. Those that cannot make payments are described as being forced into becoming drug mules, and violence against women is commonplace. Vulnerable migrants are said to be victimized and traumatized frequently throughout the migration journey.

Upon successful entry into the US, migrant asylum seekers, whether legal or undocumented, are said to face significant obstacles and barriers relative to inclusion. The US lacks developed social infrastructures necessary to facilitate cultural integration, specifically, public transit services, civic spaces for cultural exchanges, affordable housing, and devoted community resources on local levels to help foster integration. Asylum seekers within the US system often have court hearings significantly distanced from their established locations, making attendance problematic. Establishing oneself within the US is described as a lengthy and expensive process for migrants. Language barriers create significant employment challenges, particularly for indigenous migrants who speak native dialects. Few employment opportunities exist that allow migrants to develop skills and experience necessary for management or mid-level management careers.

For undocumented migrants, a pervasive inability to participate fully in society comes with numerous difficulties, often linked to lack of access to the formal economy, including the inability to obtain a driver's license, insurance, or bank account or to gain meaningful employment beyond the often manual or basic-labor work available in the shadow economy (construction, harvesting agriculture, dishwasher, hotel housekeeping, etc.). US businesses that do hire undocumented migrants often have exploitative practices, and workers hardly have any protection or recourse when faced with such abuse. Some stakeholders discuss cases where migrants are held in slave-like conditions or are not paid for their work as initially agreed upon. Migrants face discrimination, legal barriers, and political stigmatization that largely keep them in the shadows of society. Limited social mobility and reported feelings of powerlessness, fear, and discouragement were commonly mentioned themes. Migrants are described as fearful of authority and hesitant to report crimes for fear of being deported.

As migrants leave the NT, origin countries suffer economic and societal costs as a result of remittance dependence, fractured families, and stress on the remaining population that emerges from their departure. Vital generational skills are lost, creating economic vacuums that demoralize and deplete communities further. A lack of dialogue and genuine commitment among origin countries and the US, as well as the US withdrawal from the Global Compact for Safe, Orderly, and Regular Migration, is said to create additional difficulties for the people of the NT.

Overall, the US asylum process is described as detention, where individuals' lives are put on hold for extended, sometimes ambiguously indefinite periods. Shelters and detention facilities are sparsely resourced, particularly ill-equipped for stays of extended durations. Recent US policies, such as the Migration Protection Protocols (MPP), are described indignantly as prioritizing enforcement to a humanitarian fault. Once inside detention centers, it becomes difficult for migrant asylum seekers (asylees) to gain access to legal counsel and translation services often critical for successfully verifying identity and establishing the claim for asylum.

Comprehensive reform and overhauls to the US immigration system are said to be required in order to release mounting societal pressures and regional violence. Virtually every stakeholder offered harsh criticisms for current US immigration policies, with several calling for complete, systematic overhauls in order to meaningfully address the growing challenges. While opinions differed on solutions, addressing the backlog of asylum-seeking court cases is seen as absolutely critical. Creating a fair, clear, timely, and dignified process for adjudicating asylum claims is said to be a necessary priority for the US. Allowing asylum seekers to make asylum claims in their native language was also mentioned as potentially helping establish identity and expedite the process.

Better resourcing and equipping the administrative side of the US migration process was another common theme among stakeholders when making exclusion–inclusion claims. The resources identified as needed include hiring more staff to process applications and more judges to process claims, focusing on hires with social work backgrounds rather than law enforcement, eliminating red tape for law enforcement officers, and offering more technical solutions to assist in border monitoring. In sum, stakeholders describe the need to advance a holistic plan toward simplifying regular and managed migration to prevent irregular and illegal migration at all costs. For those already in the US, creating programs that provide protective status, career advancement opportunities, and a way out of the shadows of society is needed to help the US capitalize on the innovation, drive, and work ethic that a migrant workforce can bring.

Beyond logistics and policies, stakeholders also discussed the rhetorical politicization of migration when making exclusion–inclusion claims. The Trump administration's intentional rhetorical demonizing and criminalizing of the migrant community is said to have been immensely hurtful and damaging. Such rhetoric is considered unfair, degrading, and utterly political in nature. Further, such demeaning rhetoric from the nation's highest office normalizes microaggressions toward migrants across lower levels of society; racism becomes part of the migrant experience in US communities. The portrayal of migrants as rapists, job stealers, and as writ large enemies is seen as callously diminishing the contributions of migrants to the US communities that they are a part of, unnecessarily inflicting hate on an already vulnerable group that largely seeks to stay unnoticed.

The broad consensus among stakeholders was that political rhetoric surrounding migration at best served only to limit the ability of communities to reasonably consider ways to manage migration-related issues cooperatively and inclusively and at worst created a toxic fear of migrants. The rise of a so-called *Fortress America* narrative, which views the outside world with suspicion and angst was described as contributing to an inability to sensibly discuss ways to better manage migration flows and integrate migrants into communities.

Some stakeholders noted that narratives in the US concerning migration are stuck in a 1990s mentality: filled with images of Mexican agricultural workers, rather than asylum-seeking families. US citizens are seen as largely in the dark about the scope of challenges facing migrants fleeing the NT, as well as possessing little knowledge on US immigration processes. Educating US citizens about current migration challenges is seen as a way of future-proofing the US immigration system, allowing citizens to have a voice in building a more flexible immigration system.

Finally, stakeholders pointed out that words such as illegal, undocumented, alien, and refugee carry negative and, in some cases, dehumanizing exclusionary connotations. The preferred inclusive terminology mentioned by numerous stakeholders when discussing migrants was *New Americans*, simultaneously reflective of their pre-existing status as continental Americans, demonstrative of their specific newness to the US, and illustrative of the fresh start ahead of them in the land of the free.

Expanded Exclusion-Inclusion Findings

Here, the exclusion–inclusion claims made by stakeholders are categorized relative to the vantage points offered, allowing the reader to see how each group of stakeholders differs in focus.

Migrant Exclusion-Inclusion Claims

Once in the US, migrants' significant challenges related to exclusion–inclusion: lack of social infrastructure and exploitative business practices. Social infrastructure difficulties include inabilities to get a driver's license, insurance, bank account, and other factors that are "*crippling problems in terms of social mobility.*" Business exploitative practices are another major challenge.

According to migrants, there is *"little worker protection for undocumented migrants."* Even though migrants *"have options for labor, unjust treatment by employers is common."* One quote illustrates this point well: *"Sometimes businesses will hire migrants, have the work completed, and then pay them far less than agreed or not pay them at all."* Additionally, *"when businesses get in trouble for hiring undocumented migrant labor, migrants themselves lose out on pay for work they have done."*

When dealing with the US immigration bureaucracy, migrants feel scared, powerless, and discouraged. One respondent shared that the process of status changes at the US–Mexican embassy felt *"unprofessional"* as *"people [were] crammed in"* and that the process cost $17,000 in *"attorney fees and immigration fees and travel fees."* Lastly, migrants refer to the cycle of migration and violence: When *"undocumented immigrants are deported with a criminal record, [it is] making it easier for them to join the gangs."*

Migrants also briefly discuss solutions. Better administrative processes (e.g., more staff processing migrant applications, more resources, more employees with backgrounds in social work instead of law enforcement) are among the solutions. Other solutions are tied to the US leaders fostering more respect and recognition of migrant workers and communities. For example, one interviewee said, *"Fostering a sense of respect for the work that migrants do would go a long way to building relationships and easing fears."*

Policy Experts Exclusion–Inclusion Claims

Policy experts often discuss asylum difficulties in relation to exclusion–inclusion, pointing out that it is extremely difficult for asylum seekers to obtain legal help once placed in detention, which is frequently compared to prison. The problems with this system include the language barrier (i.e., inability to communicate stories/evidence inhibits qualification for asylum) and the long periods required to adjudicate their cases. Additionally, once asylum seekers are in the system, they are kept in locations other than the US, making attending immigration court hearings problematic. This further contributes to migration system challenges. As a result, only a fraction of asylum seekers are granted status. One respondent provided more details:

> People have been assaulted, kidnapped, extorted while in the program because they are essentially being forced to sit in limbo … 65,000 people have been put

through the program since 2019 and less than 1% have been granted asylum. About 600 people total have been granted asylum out of about 60,000.

Another challenge associated with exclusion–inclusion is the lack of dialogue and real commitment among countries, and the US withdrawal from the Global Compact for Safe, Orderly, and Regular Migration creates additional difficulties. Migration, according to one interviewee, is *"a regional issue and should be managed as a region. Panama, Canada, and Costa Rica should also be involved in helping NT."* Overall, most policy experts agree that migration issues need to be addressed by regional responses and demand shared commitment and cooperation globally among countries.

Policy experts are eager to offer their solutions to migration problems: cooperation and coordinated responses, economic partnerships, an expanded US role, and basic assistance. Long-term, regional and coordinated responses are at the heart of policy expert solutions. This will require cooperative partnerships among the US and origin countries. Effective economic policy should create opportunities within origin countries and provide populations with *"the ability to stay in their home countries."* Changes need to start at the community level, suggests one expert. It is necessary to establish safety and development opportunities so people will stay within their homes. Moreover, legal working contracts or *maquiladoras* may be an effective means of facilitating opportunities for education and employment and may be helpful in preventing violence. What is undeniable to policy experts is that development will require organized cooperation among developmental actors, lending institutions, civil society, and businesses in order to be effective. Additionally, economic action should be accompanied by a blend of reactive/first responder actions providing basic assistance (i.e., food, water, shelter, and security). In sum, these solutions require *"thought and foresight, and planning, and compassion, and practical flexibility."*

Since rural communities in the NT are especially vulnerable, they should be addressed with additional care, according to some policy experts. They maintain that stability and order are vital within these rural communities. It will require long-term *"real solutions toward ensuring stability,"* including *"addressing the very real issue of violence, extortion and discrimination against indigenous and farming communities."*

Policy experts are most vocal about the US' special role in solving the migration problem (at least eight of them specifically commented on this). First, experts say it is the responsibility of the US to stand up to the corruption taking place in the NT. They argue for long-term investments to tackle corruption. While organizations such as International Commission against Impunity in Guatemala (CICIG) were beneficial, there is a greater need for professional policing. As one expert comments, the US should...

> *give financial and technical assistance to NT, but also use political pressure to encourage progress addressing impunity and ensuring that there is a price to pay when progress being made to strengthen the rule of law and combat corruption is curtailed by government decisions.*

Second, the US needs a systematic overhaul of its immigration system, with the ability to rapidly adjudicate cases in a fair and dignified manner, disincentivizing immigrants without strong claims. Additionally, modifications to the system should allow asylum seekers protection and humane treatment while their claims are being processed, as well as clearly defined criteria for granting asylum, allowing faster retrieval and verification of facts to bring asylum cases to quick and fair conclusions. Policy experts are also eager to give examples of successful programs, such as the CICIG, Comprehensive Refugee Response Framework (CRRF), Family Case Management Program, and community-managed asylum programs. Additionally, policy experts call for future-proofing of the US immigration system.

One respondent put it best:

> *When we're thinking about our immigration system ... the core thing we need is to have a flexible immigration system that's future proof. You need to have an immigration system that can adjust to different types of flows, whether that be changes in legal immigration or irregular immigration. Flexibility is going to be very important for a system that can sustain itself over time.*

Academic Exclusion-Inclusion Claims

Academics spend a lot of time discussing solutions to migration, most of which relate to exclusion–inclusion criteria of the state, in particular, the US. As the scope and the nature of the migration challenges have changed over time, academics consistently call for reforms, sustainable change, and a more robust immigration process. Harsh criticisms of current US policies abound, as, for example, "*complete overhaul of migration system should be considered*" and "*take current immigration policy and crumple it up in a ball and throw it into the trash can.*" Reform is seen as inevitable, as the refusal to reform will lead to more violence and displacements. One academic closes with John Kennedy's quote: "*Those who refuse to reform make revolution inevitable.*"

Investments in the NT region, with a focus on entrepreneurship initiatives and sustainable solutions, is the most frequently mentioned theme within solutions provided by academics. Foreign investments are viewed as critical in the stabilization of these countries. These investments are best directed toward educational efforts, micro-investments into local communities, and technical assistance. Small NGOs and local organizations are positioned best at stabilizing and bolstering self-sustaining communities. As an example, one respondent shared his personal experience working with the farming community near Cuilapa, Guatemala. His project involved a partnership with the Food and Agriculture Organization of the United Nations (FAO). He said,

> *I think that what really impressed me about FAO was the fact that they were really teaching sustainable farming methods. So they would show up with their team of people. If a grower said, 'yes, I'm willing to work with you,' they said, 'well, we've got a list here of 15 or 20 different sustainable practices we'd like for you to try. Pick eight or ten of these and try it for X amount of years and then let us know.' We'll keep working with you, but we want to see what happens. Oh, my goodness. Huge difference.*

Another quote from the same participant captures notions of sustainability particularly well:

> *It's one thing to grow corn. Well, that's great. But, you know, if all you do is grow corn and then you sell it and you eat it. You're still hand to mouth, but if say a corn area could develop where they had their own mill, they could mill it, they could create flour, cornmeal, etc. Then if you added to that some kind of a system where they were going to add even more value to that product by baking it or whatever they're going to do. Oh, my goodness, the things that could happen.*

Another solution, provided by academics, is grounded in simplifying regular and managed migration in order to avoid irregular and illegal migration at all costs. They back their argument with a notion that migration is a natural process: "*people are going to move for economic resources; it is historic and natural; attempting to clamp the flow too hard causes others disruptions.*" Migration, academics say, is becoming even more important in a global system, which "*by definition has flows of people and money ... constantly.*" In order to answer the question of...

> *how do we make El Salvador, Guatemala and Honduras a better place is to allow the flow to move around and create wealth; and that wealth, some of it goes back and makes for nicer towns and nicer villages and hopefully better political systems.*

Academics are also very keen on discussing challenges and impediments to solutions. Broadly, the obstacles include harmful policies and practices, perception of migration as an unmanageable issue, and a growing number of migrants. The currently established policies are viewed as being "*not holistic,*" not "*coordinated,*" not "*multidisciplinary approaches*" that are largely "*about mitigating the symptoms of the crisis.*" The harmful practices include the use of police and military "*to go after these gangs or criminal organizations [that] has actually made things worse and has only increased violence in many respects.*" The barriers are also considered by academics as not being effective, as "*people have already made up their mind and have little options.*"

At least three responders said that the perception of migration as an unmanageable issue is a real obstacle to overcoming the problem. As one person said,

> *the perception is that it is not manageable, that it's a drain on our resources and that rhetoric seems to dominate our discourse; and it impedes us from really tackling the problem in a serious, complex way because this is a serious, complex problem.*

Another participant said that the "*leaders often exacerbate political resource conversations as finite in terms of needed human capacity (and, therefore, arguing against external labor) against that of needed material resource protection (and, therefore, arguing for rigorous enforcement of boundaries).*" The growing number of migrants is also discussed as a challenge to the proposed solutions. Several academics view resettlement as not a viable option for the current levels of global displacement because "*there is less and less willingness in the countries that could resettle them to take them.*"

Journalist Exclusion-Inclusion Claims

Administrative hurdles are the most often stated exclusion–inclusion claims. According to journalists, current US laws have profound effects on migration: legal pathways are difficult to pursue because they are costly and extremely time-consuming. Many migrants who genuinely qualify for asylum are facing a severely backlogged and overloaded system. Moreover, the zero-tolerance policy prevents migrants who entered illegally from pursuing a legal course of action. Additionally, language difficulties and cultural differences contribute to the problem. One respondent illustrated the example:

> *It's just not obvious to the people who are going through this, what of their terrible experiences are going to qualify them for asylum in a context in which people are traumatized and dealing with strangers. And in an unfamiliar country, it's very hard to ensure that all of the relevant facts will come out in sufficient time.*

Shelter Worker Exclusion-Inclusion Claims

While most of the exclusion–inclusion conversations with other stakeholders focused on illegal aspects of entry, shelter workers noted that, even when crossing legally, migrants also face major difficulties. It is a strenuous process for asylum seekers to enter the US as there are very few pathways. Additionally, the process is often very expensive, involving costs such as getting a translator, paying for bus tickets, flights, court, and so on. According to shelter workers, US policies force migrants into the shadows rather than helping them contribute to the system.

Solutions to the migration crisis need to be implemented at the grassroots level, according to shelter workers. These include both addressing violence and helping create economic opportunities. Local leaders, particularly indigenous ones, need to be included in the solution to effectively tailor the solution to local needs. It is important to focus on investing in the next generation to become entrepreneurs in sustainable businesses to both retain populations and restore the local economy.

Several programs and recommendations emerged within conversions with shelter workers. For example, the Central American Minors Affidavit of Relationship (CAM-ARO) has demonstrated effectiveness in reducing the number of unaccompanied minors arriving at the US–Mexico border by getting clearance beforehand and obtaining knowledgeable legal assistance. Naturally, another recommendation emerges—to find ways to "*better coordinate between shelters and governments.*" Shelter workers could receive more extensive training to help and advise migrants in a variety of ways. It is apparent that the current lack of communication between shelters and governments results in blind spots in the governments' decision-making, as well as contributing to the lack of assistance to shelters.

Expanding NGO work and cooperation with governments is another recommendation. According to shelter workers, NGOs are frequently stepping up to provide assistance that governments are unable or unwilling to provide, including food, shelter, and transportation to distant immigration courts. Without NGO assistance, the humanitarian problem the US would face would be considerably more serious and urgent. It is also important to note here that several shelter workers across the country refused to take part in this study due to expressed distrust, disgust, and disdain for US government officials.

Law Enforcement Exclusion-Inclusion Claims

Discussions with law enforcement focused on the outdated US policy incapable of handling current migration issues. In short, the US government isn't "*prepared for a large influx*"; the system "*is not set up for people to succeed in trying to enter the US and starting a new life*"; and "*following guidelines and due process makes [civil service] jobs difficult.*" The language barrier is also contributing to migrants' challenges once in the US:

> You're trying to get to the US, [and] what ends up happening is you get to the border, you suddenly have to apply in a language that you don't know and you [are] filling out legal documents in a language you don't know, which would be hard even in a native language.

Migration as a dehumanized and political issue is often discussed in the context of challenges and obstacles. As one respondent put it, "*You turn away the human side of the issue in favor of boiling it down to these almost inconsequential terms and titles and taking away the humanity of the issue.*" When talking about solutions to these challenges, one respondent offered his viewpoint: "*if you take away the type of stigma and the really negative view of immigration that we see a lot right now, then you can actually have an open discourse about it.*" In another quote, the same respondent addressed the lack of political will to fix the problem: "*Creating better processes for people to enter the US, but I think that type of ... mental paradigm needs to be shifted in order to actually open the door for creating these better processes.*"

Solutions to existing problems, as offered by law enforcement officers, fall into two categories: technical solutions (such as expediting technical possibilities needed to track border crossings) and personnel recommendations (such as eliminating red tape when possible and letting officers get needed information; providing more personnel; and eliminating bribery via extended background checks and good communication).

Vocational Trainer Exclusion-Inclusion Claims

Vocational trainers spent most of their time highlighting the initial challenges that migrants face in the US. Assimilating into a new country is difficult, especially with few resources, working in a low-paying job, and enduring the loss of their former community.

When first arriving in the US, migrants face a language barrier. Learning English is the first hurdle to overcome to obtain a decent job, says one vocational trainer. Vocational trainers with success in career laddering migrants argued that cities across the US should, "*...integrate a system like ours*" of teaching English to the migrants right away to help set them up for success later on. The initial cost to migrants of establishing themselves is steep. Vocational trainers see some immigrants come already financially stable, while most require assistance. According to one trainer, a system that could help with the initial upfront costs would benefit in dividends long term. The main answer to these problems is a "*program that's well thought through and is truly designed to make an immigrant self-sufficient.*" This would include a system that would help immigrants obtain a driver's license, provide education, financially stabilize, and self-diagnose other needs of migrants in trying to establish themselves.

Another challenge for migrants is obtaining employment that will develop into a career. Typically, migrants fill a position in high-demand industries because they are willing to hire these workers. As one trainer said, "*They may come and get a job, but that's not a career for them to build up on top.*" An offered solution to this problem is creating a program (or a series of localized programs) designed to develop infrastructure for migrants to become self-sufficient. Once they become self-sufficient, they can become producers in the economy.

Phenomena of Interest

As violence is cited as a primary reason for migration, stakeholders focus most prominently on phenomena that convey the scope of damages caused by gangs, cartels, and systemic corruption, as well as outlining their perspectives on addressing the respective challenges. The most notable and consistent phenomenological theme among stakeholders is that migrants fleeing from the Northern Triangle enter a vast, organized, dangerous, and often cruel human trafficking network; *"no one crosses the border without paying."* Offering solutions to this broader phenomenon are often central aspects of stakeholder responses.

Opportunities and solutions to the crisis of NT migration are most often presented around phenomena requiring long-term planning, as well as regional and international cooperation. Migration is fundamentally seen as a larger regional phenomenon requiring assistance from actors such as Canada, Panama, Costa Rica, as well as the US and Mexico. Measures aimed at reducing US–Mexico border crossings are viewed as counterproductive and limited to the short term, as cartels make more money through such restrictions and underlying catalysts become further amplified. Long-term, regional, and coordinated responses are the most commonly discussed solutions, requiring cooperative partnerships and vision.

Stakeholders note the importance of the US taking an active, and visible, stance against corruption in the region; even if such efforts are only nominal, they are seen as critically important. Economic interventions are described as requiring local-level input across all aspects of implementation. Stakeholders point out that NGOs and other organizations already working in the region should be further empowered and utilized; particularly important are investments in programs that help create entrepreneurial opportunities in the region. Change must begin at the community level, creating pockets of stability that can be further linked together economically. Facilitating opportunities for education and employment along the migratory route and as part of the migratory process can reduce transit violence and expedite integration efforts.

Addressing rural migration is seen as a more logical initial effort, rather than attempting to focus directly on gang and urban-related violence. Local leaders, particularly indigenous leaders, are described as vital to effectively tailoring program solutions to local needs. Economic interventions are said to require an accompanying blend of reactive first responder actions to provide basic assistance. In sum, a holistic, multi-layered cooperative approach among developmental actors, lending institutions, civil society, and businesses is required to effectively begin solving the NT migration crisis.

Expanded Phenomena of Interest Findings

Here, the primary phenomena of interest discussed by stakeholders are categorized relative to the vantage points offered, allowing the reader to see how the focus of each group of stakeholders differs.

Migrant Phenomenon Claims

Migrants focus mainly on the challenges along the migration route, primarily navigating the organized criminal networks. They report that the preparation/training for border crossing can take months and that migration has become "*far more dangerous in recent years.*" According to interview participants, very few people attempt the asylum option and, instead, prefer to pay a smuggler. As one migrant puts it, "*Without proper papers, a coyote is the only real option.*" Migrants clearly voice major difficulties associated with human smugglers. They discuss very organized operations by smugglers, difficulty in holding "*money transfer negotiations,*" and the likelihood of migrants being taken advantage of. They also complain about smugglers who "*kidnap and harm the people*" and about significant price increases in smuggling services ("*from $2000 in early 2000s to more than $8000; up to $12,000 for aircraft passage*").

Policy Experts' Phenomenon Claims

Policy experts discuss smugglers and media as major contributors to migration challenges. The abundance of wrongful information perpetrated by smugglers and media has led to a lot of people being easily misled. As one interviewee said, "*Media attention increased the ability of smugglers to spread false rumors and drive migration numbers up.*" Another challenge is that migrants are fearful of authority and are hesitant to report crimes for fear of being deported. Programs that address this issue by allowing special protective status if impacted by crime are one way of mitigating this concern.

As violence is cited as a primary reason for migration, a focus on stopping gangs and cartels seems like a natural solution. However, policy experts maintain that cartels are extremely difficult to counter and defeat. Cartels in many ways "*can be viewed as effectively a business; they act like a business and operate as such. The big difference is that they use violence and are completely willing to do horrific, awful, horrible things to keep money flowing.*" Tightening the US–Mexico border controls is viewed as counterproductive to mitigation efforts, as cartels make more money through fewer people crossing. One interviewee expanded on this notion:

> *Not surprisingly, supply and demand says that as the US government has made it more and more difficult to cross the border in recent years, the costs have gone up because the cartels recognize that tighter borders are better business.*

Mass migration also leaves its negative imprint on origin countries. As migrants leave, their nations incur economic and societal costs as a result of remittance dependence, fractured families, and stress on the remaining population that emerges from their departure. Experts warn that many communities are left without "*vital generational skills.*"

Academic Phenomenon Claims

The phenomenon claims of academics centered on psychological, economic, and social impacts of migration. Psychological impacts are associated with voids that migrated populations leave within their families. A very pronounced phenomenon is "*fatherless communities.*" It is especially prevalent in Guatemala, where some communities "*have been gutted of males or other folks that are critical for the stability and development of those communities.*" According to academics, families often report that "*even though we're better off economically than we've ever been, it just really was not worth it to be separated from our families like that in order to move ahead.*" Suicides are among other psychological impacts discussed.

Migrants also contribute to economic vacuums within their home communities "*that would be difficult to restore or regain after so many people have left or were planning on leaving.*" Additionally, displacements are often associated with loss of skills. This phenomenon is best captured by one respondent: "*Displaced people do not have opportunity to thrive economically, a knowledge gap is created; skills are lost to societies. When returned home, they lack skills and education."*

Migration has tremendous social impacts, especially for youth and women. Within the region, women are often used as a form of currency, and youth are *"targeted and threatened to join gangs or forced into relationships with gang members."* When pursuing migration, most people are unwilling to cut ties with their home communities, and *"if they do find themselves having to leave permanently for various security reasons, they're really keen on keeping those kinds of kinship and community ties alive and vibrant through this trans-national space."*

Journalists' Phenomenon Claims

When journalists discuss the major phenomena associated with migration, they are keen to point to physical and psychological hardships along the route. Migrants entering the US after crossing the border illegally are often injured (snakebites, broken legs, etc.), dehydrated, and malnourished. Young women and children, in particular, are also prone to physical abuses along the trail. One respondent cites RAICES, a legal counsel organization that reports that 60% of minors are sexually abused on the journey along the border. Additionally, psychological traumas, caused by border crossings as well as violence suffered under gangs, have a profound impact on migrants' well-being. For example, one journalist described a woman who could not utter her name in front of the judge because she *"broke down.... [and] was so unprepared to talk about the death of her husband. That's something that requires several months of therapy."*

The criminality along the border route is also discussed at length. Criminal enterprises are a major problem, according to journalists, and migrants are described as *"commodities for the cartels."* Essentially, criminal networks act as border gatekeepers since they largely control who gets in and out. They make migrants pay and send large groups toward a specific location to distract border patrol attention to allow smuggling to take place on the side. Additionally, migrants are forced to carry drugs across the border in exchange for payments.

Shelter Workers' Phenomenon Claims

Shelter workers present migrants as an extremely vulnerable group and consider it to be one of the biggest phenomena associated with migration. When crossing illegally, migrants are often brought into a situation of labor trafficking. As one interviewee shared, they *"were essentially held as slaves, ... kept in this little house, no heat, no running water while they worked as much as possible over 12-hour days on construction projects."* Another respondent shared that he had heard of *"countless stories of women who are sexually assaulted on their way from the Northern Triangle to the US."*

Shelter workers also extensively discussed COVID-19 as a distinct phenomenon impacting migrants. Consistently throughout 2020, COVID-19 complications forced caregivers at various shelters to transition from *"face-to-face interactions to remote assistance,"* making it significantly harder for migrants to receive health care. COVID-19 has also forced shelters to operate at reduced capacity, both in terms of staffing and migrants, while health locations have fewer staff and longer wait times to dispense care. Fears of transmission have prompted countries to close their borders, while shelters are unable to help migrants fill out government paperwork to receive healthcare. This results in migrants being trapped in a country or region with significant barriers to health care access, and the lack of contact with family raises further anxiety among migrants.

Law Enforcement's Phenomenon Claims

Law enforcement officers dwelled on the challenges of migration. They referred to it as a difficult process (hard to plan, costly, and highly dangerous). High costs are associated with the asylum process, hiring translators, paying for transportation to court date(s) for hearings related to their cases in various US cities, and paying cartels, gang members, and/or smugglers (coyotes). If migrants cannot pay, cartels use them as drug mules and hold them to ransom until all the money is received. If migrants die during their journey, cartels extort their families for the money.

Law enforcement officers also discuss impacts of migration on civilians. For example, they mention farmers and ranchers losing livestock due to cartels breaching fences, civilians at risk of targeting by pseudo-cops, and cartels driving through people's property and causing major damage.

Vocational Trainers' Phenomenon Claims

Vocational trainers also focus on the phenomenon of psychological trauma associated with migration. After leaving their home country and resettling, migrants experience feelings of isolation and alienation. These individuals find themselves without a community or sense of belonging. One vocational trainer said that the classes she taught had morphed into a community; students came to class because they felt like they belonged to a group of people. The feeling of alienation for immigrants is similar to that of a home renter—the feeling of being evicted at any moment without notice. Without the sense of "home," there is a lack of motivation to participate and contribute. However, when there is a feeling of community, it *"helps people feel successful"* and spurs them to continue on.

Additional Themes and Conclusions

The interview data provided many other broad thematic takeaways that helped present a larger picture of migration. The larger perspective painted is that of significant regional instability, driven by elite and institutional corruption that has stripped away the ability of NT states to offer protection against criminal exploitation of citizens, respond to financial and environmental crises, or offer needed social welfare programs. The scope of the problem presented is said by stakeholders to require cooperative solutions that are both regional and international. The major concluding themes across each stakeholder group are presented next.

Migration stakeholders often mention an increasingly hostile political rhetoric presenting migrants as enemies. As one respondent said, *"rhetoric criminalizing undocumented workers as violent is hurtful and damaging."* Such *"unfair"* rhetoric originates within the US administration, bringing *"microaggressions of overt racist comments as part of the experience in the community"* and further perpetrating discrimination against migrants. One respondent presents his idea of a dream—a world where *"we would have a license to drive; a renewable permit that is paid for in exchange for a feeling of tranquility; without fear of being taken advantage of and without fear of ICE deportation."*

Policy experts often noted the ineffectiveness of US information campaigns. According to one interviewee, potential migrants learn more about the migration process from social networks than from official information campaigns. They see both good and bad experiences, and often, the *"individual exceptionalism"* mentality wins. As one expert puts it, *"My experience will be different.... That won't happen to me. That happened to that other person, not me."* Another respondent reported that focusing on the *"losing your life"* narrative within information campaigns is ineffective. Rather, information campaigns should focus on the low chances of succeeding on the migration journey. Another policy expert shared that information campaigns can be helpful to combat disinformation spread by smugglers. Specifically, it might be fruitful to explain to potential migrants how the asylum system works and that it is *"not really set up for people who just had [their] small business extorted."* However, this is not the viewpoint that was shared by all policy experts we interviewed. As one respondent observed, *"the [US] policy changes so often that the information campaigns are ineffective."* He further added on behalf of migrants: *"that was our experience six months ago, but how do we know if that's going to be our experience now?"*

Academics highlighted the impact on migration when presented as a political issue to the public. As one respondent put it, *"this issue is demagogued, it's politicized, is used for some political gain."* This trend only compounds the real challenges of migration, making the situation worse. Political rhetoric on migration is seen as *"short-term oriented and causing long-term problems,"* with US media contributing to further polarization. The real wall, according to academics, is the US political situation that *"prevents an evolution on migration discussions and approaches."* Two major themes emerge in the discussion of rhetoric that surrounds migration: the rhetoric of "migrants as enemies" and the rhetoric of "Fortress America." According to academics, the "migrants as enemies" narrative often originates within US administration communications, as well as news media, and contributes to the isolationist policies that other wealthy nations adopt in following the US lead. Such rhetoric is also counter-productive to solving the larger migration problem. Academics are vocal for the *"need to eliminate narratives that migrants are an inherent danger"* and *"need to eliminate these zero-sum game narratives."* Instead, they promote that the *"threat narratives [are to be] replaced with cooperative regional narratives."* The rhetoric of "Fortress America" is explained as the *"underlying idea that the world will eventually implode and we need to barricade ourselves in before that happens."* The "Fortress America" rhetoric, a fear-driven narrative, is seen as harmful to solving the migration problem because it *"prevents ... a will to address underlying stability issues in Central America."*

Journalists expressed their concern for the information ecosystem that migrants have. They share, for example, that migrants do not understand what asylum is and how to apply for it. As one journalist put it, *"people think that asylum is [something that] you ask for. And as long as your intentions are good and you're here to work, we'll see that you're a good person and I'll let you in."* Information on who qualifies for asylum and how the asylum process works may be beneficial for potential migrants.

Shelter workers highlighted the need for less harmful rhetoric toward migrants. They shared that migrants often complain about how unwanted they feel within the US, how they are portrayed as stealing jobs and being "*shadow rapist(s).*" Alternatively, as one shelter worker said, a more productive and preferable term would be "*New Americans.*" Vocational trainers further pointed out that the words "refugee," "illegal," and "undocumented" carry negative connotations. One vocational trainer said that members of society were labeling them as undocumented, even if they were not. To combat this harsh rhetoric, vocational trainers suggest calling these individuals "*New American.*" There is no room to misinterpret this label; the term simply means "*...they are American but new to the country.*" Changing this language would open up society's "*... perspective of that person and their thoughts about them.*"

Law enforcement officers had one major primary narrative associated with migration as a whole: "*America as a country of immigrants.*" As one respondent puts it,

> *I think it needs to be the United States policy and my priority to welcome these people and to continue building upon being a great nation by embracing other thought processes and cultures and coming together to create something new and incredible.*

In conclusion, while the macro-level complexities of migration may indeed be staggering to assess, the more micro vantages offered here demonstrate several concrete and addressable facets of migration that could, at least from a ground level perspective, make significant impacts on the magnitude of the crisis. More importantly, the interviews demonstrate the common areas of concern (e.g., organized crime, outdated migration policies, backlogged courts) and their associated impacts between the stakeholder groups.

REFERENCES

McCormack, C. (2004). Storying stories: a narrative approach to in-depth interview conversations. *International Journal of Social Research Methodology*, *7*(3), 219–236. https://doi.org/10.1080/13645570210166382

Witz, K. G., Goodwin, D. R., Hart, R. S., & Thomas, H. S. (2001). An essentialist methodology in education-related research using in-depth interviews. *Journal of Curriculum Studies*, *33*(2), 195–227. https://doi.org/10.1080/00220270119026

## CHAPTER 4

News Media, Narrative Divergence

On June 16, 2015, Donald Trump rode an escalator down to a packed lobby in Trump Tower on Fifth Avenue in New York to officially announce his candidacy for the president of the US (Kruze, 2019). In doing so, he gave a speech laying out his platform, to which immigration policy took center stage. Lamenting that America no longer experienced "victories anymore," while making the racist claim that Mexico was intentionally sending "drugs," "crime," and "rapists" across the US border into America, Trump warned US audiences more broadly of migrants "coming from all over South America" to take jobs away from Americans, as well as of those coming "probably from the Middle East," thereby tacitly invoking fears of "Islamic terrorism." His solution was a simple, albeit oft-repeated one within US politics: build a wall. But, unlike the ones suggested by past politicians, his would be "a great wall," and one in which he would "have Mexico pay for" (Time, 2015). Although "build the wall" became one of his campaign's mantras, repeated by his followers at his political rallies, throughout Trump's four years in office only 15 miles of new fencing was created with US taxpayers, not Mexico, paying for it (Rogers & Bailey, 2020).

Despite the uniquely flagrant jingoistic flare of Trump's border security rhetoric, his general message and emotional ornamentation reflects a common trope, and recurring problem, of migration policy rhetoric. As Slaven and Boswell (2019) argue, immigration policy is particularly susceptible to symbolic policy-making; that is, the use of cosmetic policy adjustments to signal values and intent, instead of substantive measures to address the cause of concern. Nowhere is this more pronounced than in measures to combat irregular migration, which has become part of what Cvajner and Sciortino (2010) call a "complex symbolic discourse" (p. 390). Indeed, despite the failure of traditional migration policies and the salience of the topic in today's global politics, substantive progress toward immigration reform has been slow and patchy.

Given the importance of media in shaping public opinion on state policy, more broadly, and migration policy, specifically, this chapter sets out to examine national media narratives discussing migration in US, Mexican, and NT media over the past 20 years. In doing so, we argue that a narrative approach allows us to locate recurring plotlines stymieing coordination on migration reform while also enabling the identification of areas for possible transcendence toward cooperative understanding and action. As Carey (2008) contends, mass media serves not merely to transmit information but also as a ritual whereby a particular worldview is portrayed and confirmed through generally repeating plotlines or moral lessons, with such stories binding readers into a socially constructed common culture. From this perspective, news media can be understood as presenting the cultural scripts of the state, with such scripts coming to narratively define migrants' identities, behaviors, and motives for migration, while also presenting the state's identity and its routine responses in reaction to migration issues. Such routine state responses are evident from past research showing that embedded in journalists and elites' framing of migration are storylines coalescing discussion of migration through deterrence-oriented narratives in contrast to humanitarian ones, as well as examples of public discourse becoming mired in plotlines emphasizing the illegality of migration through a single-minded focus on undocumented immigrants (Jones-Correa & de Graauw, 2013; Steinhilper & Gruijters, 2018).

While such narratives may provide cognitive stability for individuals and political collectives regarding their imagined fears or anxieties toward migration, they can also result in attachment to routine ways of managing and discussing migration issues by placing migrants in positions of the "other" (Cash & Kinnvall, 2017; Kinnvall, 2004). The consequence of such rigid, unreflexive repetition of these enduring plotlines can be the inhibition of new, creative ways to address the vicissitudes of political communities' environments (Kinnvall & Mitzen, 2018) and thus requires comparison and critique in order to create change. This reflexivity is especially needed, in that, as Boswell and Badenhoop (2019) argue, little research has focused on state ignorance—the areas where states lack knowledge relevant to addressing social problems. Indeed, Boswell and Badenhoop found this to be the case with immigration policy, in particular, demonstrating how public authorities in Germany and UK problematically responded to immigration through denial and resignation.

To alleviate detrimentally ossified narratives of ignorance and/or exclusion—such as plotlines of migrants as threats or burdens to society or simply opportunistic individuals easily deterred by beefing up border security irrespective of their reasons for migrating—new, transcendent narratives are required. Indeed, while simple, powerful messages influence public opinion on global policy issues, they can also undermine cooperative goals by minimizing the space for dialogue among stakeholders. As the Migration Policy Organization explains, large-scale, unanticipated migration has demonstrated the limitations of managing migrant flows unilaterally, requiring states to cooperate through multilateral means (Newland, 2019). Focusing on the discursive elements of policy discussions by identifying, analyzing, and synthesizing publics' construction of persuasive arguments and counter-arguments from both national and transnational media can provide feedback for government and inter-government organizations to reflexively understand how their actions are understood and thus holds the potential for the constitution of communities with a shared purpose and meaning (Proedrou & Frangonikolopoulos, 2012).

The requirement of shared meaning is present, especially given today's global media ecology. Although today's globalized world has brought individuals, civil society actors, and governments closer than ever before, creating a global networked society enabling transnational actors to organize and address issues of common concern (Castells, 2008), globalization's fracturing effects have led to national media systems serving more narrow interests of the state (Flew et al., 2016; Flew, 2020). Unfortunately, studies on immigration in the Americas reflects this latter perspective, with research taking the perspective of host nation media (Palau-Sampio, 2018) with few comparative analyses outside of Western media contexts. As Cooley et al. (2022) warn, viewing migration from the NT and Mexico from a national framework discerning tactical policies to deter it is both shortsighted and overlooks its transnational nature and causes, especially when such coverage ignores reporting from the nations in which migration is occurring.

Addressing these areas of concern, in addition to answering the call for comparative large-scale analysis of media coverage (Gurevitch & Blumler, 2004), this chapter analyzes US, Mexican, and NT media narratives about migration over the past two decades. Not only is empirical research exploring how news media describe migration and the manner in which it has shifted over time underdeveloped (Harris & Gruenewald, 2020), but also, we argue, represents an important first step in understanding the lack of coordinated progress on migration policy. The remainder of this chapter lays out how we propose to identify such narratives, the summary of our results, and—most importantly—a critique and discussion of the narratives present in NT, Mexican, and US media. Here, in this final section, we comment on the differences in causal claims, themes of exclusion–inclusion, phenomenon or topics of interests, and the implications regarding the constraints and overlays of possible imagined outcomes associated with migration policy-making.

Method

According to Oates et al. (2020), narrative analysis is more of an art than a science. Thus, despite the availability of multiple avenues for analysis—ranging from rhetorical textual analyses to qualitative thematic approaches—big data has opened up the possibility for identifying and summarizing larger trends (Oates et al., 2020). Nonetheless, the gains made by algorithmic assessment of news discourse often come from more narrow, pre-set configurations. To offset these costs, while maintaining some fidelity of making broader claims to similarly repeating statistical linguistic patterns in news coverage, we offer a unique approach to examining NT, Mexican, and US news reports over the past 20 years. Thus, whereas the next chapter explores more of the structural patterns and shifts in the construction of migration-related news coverage, this chapter tries to identify the broader sense-making elements of the narrative themes present in the news discourse from these nations.

Our narrative analysis comes in two forms and divides the reporting into four time periods based on major developments in US policy discussion related to migration. Time Period 1 includes discussions one year before and after Congress's passing of the 2000 Legal Immigration Family Equity Act. Time Period 2 includes the 2005 to 2007 US House and Senate debates on immigration. Time Period 3 spans one year before and after the 2012 DACA and 2013 Gang of Eight debates. Finally, Time Period 4 represents coverage more broadly from 2015 to 2019, representing the lead-up to Donald Trump's presidency and most of his time in office.

Narrative themes were first identified by conducting key word in context (KWIC) analyses of the top 75 parts of speech where the term migrant/immigrant occurred by time period and region. These were then qualitatively grouped by two coders into the five constituent parts of a narrative (act, agent, scene, instrument, purpose/motive) to determine the narrative theme present in the entire corpus of articles for that country and time period. To corroborate these findings, while also leveraging additional insight into the narrative themes present, we conducted a second analysis by employing machine learning topic modeling algorithms. Here, articles from each time period and country/region were categorized into six clusters, which were then qualitatively analyzed by taking the top 60 exemplar windows composing the six clusters to determine the predominate narrative themes present. For an extended discussion of our methodology, see Chapter 2. In the next section, we present the results of our two narrative analyses with emphasis placed on how the narrative components shifted over time.

Mexican Media Narratives

Mexico Time Period 1

The primary agents within Mexican media narratives from Time Period 1 focus on undocumented and illegal immigrants from Mexico but also include some mentioning of CA migrants and US and Mexican government authorities. Mexican media narratives focus singularly on the economic reasons for migration, with migrants crossing the US border in increasing numbers to find work in the US and send remittances to support their families in Mexico.

Mexico P1

Key agents: Undocumented and illegal Mexican migrants/immigrants (also referred to as people or groups); US and Mexico, government authorities (INM, Felipe de Jesus Preciado Coronado, regional delegates, police), President Fox; Central Americans, civil organizations, polleros

Scene: Migrants crossing border, states, area; increases in numbers; Journey (desert, dangerous, face poor conditions and heat)

Acts: Crossing, sending/receiving (remittances), work

Instrument: worker programs, remittances; bilateral meetings, cooperation, agreements; police involvement

Purpose: Work (economic opportunities to support family in Mexico); provide protection or opportunities for migrants

Narrative clusters in Time Period 1 revolve around efforts by the Mexican government to enforce migration laws and reform policies combating migration. US–Mexico cooperation was viewed as necessary for effectively combating migration from Mexico and CA into the US, while American society remained prejudiced against Mexican migrants. Causes reported for migration revolved around economic and social factors, with migrants traveling in search of a better life. The travails in doing so, however, were described as requiring policies to recognize migrants' human dignity and provide fair treatment.

#	Description of Cluster Themes (whole article)
1	**Coordination of Mexican government agencies taking steps to prevent undocumented migrant flows**: Large number of Central Americans traveling through Mexico, necessitating mitigation strategies that include keeping the "human side in mind" aiming to limit migrant discomfort and deportations to place of origin. Notes of North American migrants treated differently than CA. Mexican citizens are sometimes victims of CA migration. Challenges to Mexican mitigation strategies include conflict among bureaucracies and some corruption issues.
2	**Mexico considering reforms to policies aimed at combating migration**: Reports of larger numbers of CA migrants coming passing through Mexico to US, with reporting of numerous arrests made. Calls for more resources to strengthen Mexico's borders and more preventive actions and campaigns to prevent migration to US. New policies described as needed to include a focus on guaranteeing respect and human rights of migrants.
3	**Mexican government's inability to prevent migration and safeguard human dignity of migrants**: Mexican government suffers from corruption, which impedes its ability to manage migration in a humane manner. Migrants described as drowning in rivers, burned in deserts, freezing in mountain ranges, and suffocating or mutilated on railroads. Migrants deceived by border patrol and coyotes. Migrants looking for better life but are returned to Mexico isolated, wounded, hungry, humiliated, and abused all without any recourse; while Americans discriminate against them.
4	**Difficulties of US–Mexican agency collaboration on migration policy**: US failed to request Mexico to participate in operation "International Crossroads," which aimed to detain illegal immigrants and "polleros" or coyotes. Mexican government downplayed its lack of involvement, suggesting some domestic backlash at US not including Mexico.

5	**Evidence of US–Mexican cooperation and understanding in addressing migration**: Visit by US ambassador and discussions of US and Mexican government officials reporting on common concerns and reflection of US–Mexico relationship. US described as concern for fighting migration at its border while understanding that Mexicans have the right to leave their country but not to enter another country. CA migration hurts Mexican society, threatening its sovereignty and corrupting government officials through bribery. Concerns that US believes all migrants are Mexican. Recognition that amnesty is a sensitive issue to US public while also affirming that US public opinion toward Mexican immigrants in US is becoming more positive. Drivers of migration explained as resulting from political oppression, instability, and violence but also demands for cheap labor from US. Solutions to migration require policies recognizing human dignity and fair treatment of migrants and their unbearable social conditions and valid aspirations for a better life. Solutions must come from collective responsibility of US and Mexico in addressing causes. Policies should not approach migration from cold, rigid tactics of prosecutions.
6	**Hope for US–Mexico close relations**: US and Mexico described as having the potential to be "allies" in fight against drug trafficking, advancement of human rights and democracy, stemming flow of migrants. Mutual cooperation can enable both countries to prosper, although American prejudices charactering all Mexicans as corrupt, drug dealers, or threats to US security undermine cooperation. US needs to approach the issue from principles of self-determination and national sovereignty.
7	**Global migration concerns**: Mexican agencies coordinating and planning ways to handle migration issues broadly, including the need to support Mexican communities abroad, need for transparency, and anti-globalization protests (negative characterizations of World Economic Forum, IMF, etc.).
8	**Elian Gonzales controversy**—balanced reporting of US and Cuban interests: Informational reports on the legal status of this case. President Clinton reported as taking personal action. US is recognized for rescuing and able to take care for Elian, with reports suggesting US is genuinely concerned for him. Nonetheless, Elian's return to Cuba symbolizes a moral and legal issue.

Mexico Time Period 2

Mexican media narratives in Time Period 2 continue to revolve around the economic motives of migration but widened their discussion to include larger numbers of US and Mexican governmental institutions and agencies enforcing migration laws as well as increased discussion of CA migrants and undocumented children. Here, the scene now included vivid depictions of migrants' journey, viewed as risky and dangerous, leading to migrant deaths, with more migrants having already established themselves and living in the US. While key acts, instruments, and goals remain finding jobs or work in the US to send remittances back to families in Mexico, migrants now also experience significant abuse, especially at the hands of employers in the US. Migrants' motivations to enter the US still included the pursuit of a better life, but also now human rights.

Mexico P2

Key agents: Undocumented (immigrant, migrant, workers, people, children, Central Americans, illegal); government (US and Mexican authorities, federal, municipal, US Senate, National Guard, Mexican National Institute of Migration); Presidents Fox and Bush; state, federal, and municipal authorities

Scene: Description of journey (area, desert, rural, cities, through Mexico); locations (California, Texas, Milwaukee); journey as risky, dangerous, deaths; migrants already established, existing, living, working in US/abroad; US/Mexico borders

Acts: sending remittances, working, abuse, death; human trafficking, violations, labor rights; Migratory flow/cross borders; ongoing studies/reports

Instrument: remittances, work, programs: temporary work, visas; construction of border wall; policies to stop illegal migratory flows; investment

Purpose: economic and social development, better life, financial support for families, jobs/work, opportunity, human rights; American Dream; protect human rights; national security

Narrative clusters in Time Period 2 revolve primarily around US–Mexican relations, with Mexico unable to defend migrant rights, attempts to coordinate with the US on policies mitigating migration, and the need to reduce the wage gap between the US and Mexico—which is reportedly the primary cause of Mexican migration to the US. Within these discussions, US immigration policies are reported as flawed, with US politicians focusing on border security—viewed as failing to stop migration by simply pushing migrants to take more dangerous routes to cross the border. Mexican authorities are reported as actively enforcing migration laws, including the arrest of migrants, coyotes, and gangs; but calls for new legislation are made in order to incentivize non-Mexican migrants to return to their countries of origin as well as policies providing protection of migrant workers and families.

Mexico 2 Clusters		
#	%	Description of Cluster Themes
0	11	INM arresting and charging migrants, including "polleros," gangs, Chinese, and South Korean. Emphasis placed on the legal justifications and trial of migrants. INM working in concert with multiple Mexican state and local authorities and courts.
1	27	Changing demographic characteristics of Mexican migration into the US. Enhanced economic and educational affordances in Mexico have shifted Mexican migrants into the US as becoming increasingly educated. Now, young Mexican people and women are migrating to the US. Mexican migrants moving to new areas in the US, such as New York and Raleigh.
2	11	Failure of US government to pass immigration reform. President Bush promised immigration reform, but Congressional Republicans blocked the bill. Republicans called the bill amnesty, want to criminalize undocumented workers and strengthen border security. Key elements of the bill include providing temporary employment visas for migrants filling jobs Americans don't want and legalization of undocumented immigrants currently in the US.
3	10	US investment in surveillance technology, additional fencing, and more border agents along Arizona border, resulting in Mexican migrants traversing increasingly inhospitable areas still left unguarded, resulting in record deaths and dehydration. US volunteers—The Minute Men—monitoring the border and "hunting" migrants. Migrants will continue to come according to labor needs of US economy.

(*Continued*)

Mexico 2 Clusters		
#	%	Description of Cluster Themes
4	3	Migration groups in Mexico and the US criticizing Mexican government for its inability to protect undocumented immigrants traveling to the US, as well as Latin American governments. Migrants will continue to cross the border, whether risking crossing the desert or using polleros regardless of US immigration reform, which only benefits skilled labor. Migration is related to human development, specifically poverty.
5	38	Criticism of Mexican authorities for being servile to US immigration interests and unable to defend Mexican interests. Mexico failing to reduce the wage gap between the two countries, which is identified as the primary cause of migration. Mexican government must support legislation providing incentives for migrants to return to country of origin, as well as mitigating undocumented immigrants from third countries and OTMs (other than Mexican), including cooperation with the US on extradition. Mexico needs to make a "frontal attack" on human trafficking gangs. It must protect migrant workers and families and eliminate child labor domestically.

Mexico Time Period 3

Time Period 3 narratives continue to mention undocumented migrants from Mexico and CA as well as a variety of Mexican and US government authorities enforcing migration laws, but shift to prominently include human traffickers and organized crime, as well as civil society and human rights organizations. The scene in which migration occurs continues to include descriptions of the journey and its difficulties but now focuses on increasing flows of CAs coming through Mexico as conditions decline in CA countries. Acts now focus on human rights violations and crimes committed against migrants, including kidnappings, extortion, and rape as well as enforcement mechanisms such as detentions, deportations, and family separations. Migrants' purpose for migration no longer revolves singularly on economic or employment related reasons but still includes a broader search for a better life, supporting families at home, and pursuit of the American Dream, as well as securing human rights, dignity, and respect while US authorities view migration as a national security issue.

Mexico P3

Key agents: Undocumented (immigrant, migrant, people, young/children, Central Americans, foreigner)
Government (US and Mexican authorities, El Salvador federal, state, municipal, police, agents, Mexican National Institute of Migration, ministries); human traffickers, organized crime, gangs; civil society organizations, NGOs, Human Rights Commission, IACHR

Scene: US/Mexico border; Description of journey: through Mexico (Central Americans), difficulty of journey, increase flows, declining conditions in Central America, migratory stations

Acts: Crimes committed against migrants (kidnapping, extortion, rape); Human rights violations (trafficking, gang violence, sexual violence, organized crime); Detention, deportation of migrants; Sheltering and support of migrants

Instrument: Deterrence instruments and government policies (detaining, enforcement of laws, family separation, wall); Shelters/stations for migrants; Trains; Remittances

Purpose: American Dream; new life; protect/defend human rights, dignity, respect; supporting family and children; national security

Narrative clusters revolve around decreases in Mexican migrants and large increases in CA migrants. Mexican immigration is reported as hitting all-time lows as increased employment, health, and education opportunities arise in Mexico in combination with enforcement efforts, decreasing the relative benefits of migrating to the US. Nonetheless, CA migration through Mexico to the US is reported as rising substantially due to CA countries' severe economic conditions. Mexican media narratives note that despite significant arrests and enforcement of migration policies by Mexico and the US, as well as the dangers of journeying to the US, CA migrants remain committed to migrating to the US as they would rather die on the journey than starve at home. CA migrants are depicted as vulnerable populations facing significant violence en route to the US and in Mexico. As such, Mexican media report the need for US–Mexican cooperation in comprehensively developing responses that guarantee security and respect for the dignity of migrants.

Mexico 3 Clusters		
#	%	Description of Cluster Themes
0	9	Obama administration leading bipartisan effort at comprehensive immigration reform, although "classic" differences between Republicans and Democrats remain. The reform would include measures for a path to citizenship, border security, and labor controls designed to verify status of migrant workers. House Republicans blocking the measure, dominated by a small, narrow-minded group not interested in governing, but sabotaging the measure. Immigration reform will benefit US economy and reduce federal debt. Latinos viewed as key voting constituency for Democrats and Republicans.
1	14	CA migrants traveling through Mexico via train and stopping at shelters in Mexico. Conflict and violence emerging between Mexican citizens and CA migrants at migrant shelters, leading to shut down of shelters. Mexican residents remain hostile toward undocumented people, viewing shelters as causing safety concerns. Catholic diocese running migrant shelters call for government support to protect and defend migrants' human rights. Civil society and activists claim Mexican authorities have criminalized and delegitimized defending of migrant rights. Migrants viewed as vulnerable population, facing violence. Migrants committed to remaining in shelter locations, despite Mexican authorities' relocation efforts, because of the dangerous journey. Families and children have no other place to sleep and lack basic goods.
2	26	Increasing flow of migration to Mexico, including from CA and Mexican return migration. Return migration up 200% caused by increasing deportations and forced return, loss of jobs, and deterioration of living conditions due to US economic recession. CA migration caused by bad economic conditions, with CA migrants preferring to die on the journey to the US rather than starve at home. Activists calling for new laws preventing criminalization of migration.

3	38	Increased employment, health, and education, in addition to improvements in law enforcement, leading to less Mexican migration to the US, with Mexican immigrants even considering returning to Mexico. US–Mexico relations need to focus on economy, investment, and job creation, while Mexican government needs to demonstrate commitment to fighting crime and structural issues, leading to violence generated by crime. US–Mexican cooperation must move beyond simple security concerns and include comprehensive political responses guaranteeing security and respect for dignity of migrants. US and Mexico cooperating on migration via repatriation points. Thousands of CA migrants requesting transit through Mexico to US.
4	9	Multiple Mexican authorities cooperating on arresting numerous instances of undocumented CA migrants and human traffickers in Mexico. Mexican authorities successfully placing migrants in custody, including repatriation. However, Mexico's INM reports it is impossible for the US to deport 300,000 foreigners to Mexico each year, especially as more and more CA migrants attempt to transit through Mexico to the US.
5	5	INM returning CA migrants to place of origin. Migrants face perils at home, lacking opportunities to have a decent life. Mexican civil society organizations pressuring Mexican government to protect and respect life and integrity of migrants. Need for policies in favor of migrants, including broader dialogue, beyond just security, to include education.

Mexico Time Period 4

Time Period 4 narratives continue to include US and Mexican government authorities and institutions as key agents, albeit with President Trump specifically mentioned, with criminal groups and civil society actors still prominent. The scene in which migration occurs, however, turns more negative, with emphasis on overcrowded shelters and migrants' poor living conditions. The journey remains characterized as risky and difficult, with a shift toward CA migrants traversing rivers and crossing borders. Acts narrow to migrants crossing and arriving at borders as well as deterrence policies arresting and separating children. Mexican media also reports a greater focus on the need to protect migrants who require humanitarian care, medical treatment, food, and shelter. The reported goals for migrants still include pursuing work to support their families but also focus on migrants seeking asylum and protection, stemming from the political situation in the home countries. Thus, Mexican media reports CA migrants as increasingly using caravans, buses, and shelters on their journey through Mexico to the US while characterizing US policies as racist, xenophobic, and anti-humanitarian; especially as the US steps up child separation policies and places migrants in cages.

Narrative clusters during this time revolve around the following issues: first, US–Mexico relations, specifically Trump and Obrador's meeting, with coverage claiming that Trump's policies cause negative repercussions

Mexico P4

Key agents: Government (Mexican, US, President Trump, Honduras, El Salvador, Guatemala, Federal, National Guard, state and local and municipal authorities, National Migration Institute); Central/Latin American (migrants, families, countries); Criminal groups; Civil society

Scene: Overcrowded shelters; poor living conditions (violence, economic, vulnerable, trafficking); journey (risk, difficult); Central American and US borders; Journey (leaving CA, arriving in Mexico; borders, rivers)

Acts: Migration (crossing, arrival, entering, come); deterrence policies (child separation, arrests); protection of migrants (support, humanitarian care, medical, food, shelter, refuge)

Instrument: Caravans, buses; Policies (US) to stem flow (child separation, caging, arrests); shelters; Central American development; economic (remittance, visas)

Purpose: Asylum, seeking (refuge, protection, political situation, life, family, work, health provisions); reaching the US; Human rights; US policies (racist, xenophobic, anti-humanitarian); shelters providing protection and aid; supporting families (remittance, support)

regarding migration and ignores its root causes. Second, and relatedly, Trump strong-arming Obrador to take additional steps to prevent CA migration into the US. Third, Mexico actively enforcing migration policies but maintaining that migrants need to be treated with respect, with consideration on protecting their human rights and supporting asylum claims. Fourth, harsher policies reported as failing to address the social and economic conditions underlying CA migration. And, finally, CA migrants facing humanitarian and human rights violations, with child separation policies viewed as inhumane.

Mexico 4 Clusters		
#	%	Description of Cluster Themes
0	7	Migration is a recurring problem despite deportations from US and Mexico (INM). Migrants are peaceful but receive little support.
1	19	CA migrants travel via caravan across Mexico because legal requests for travel are too slow or are rejected, prompting arrest and deportation by INM. INM enforces immigration law, coordinated among multiple levels of government, including US.
2	5	Mexican President Manuel Obrador discussing with US President Trump on US–Mexican relations, including managing migration. Mexico does not have a migration crisis, but CA does. General agreement regarding cooperative relations with the US to enforce stricter immigration policies; however, Mexico emphasizes need to address root causes in addition to reinforcing border security. Mexico maintains need to treat migrants with respect, protect them, apply law without violating human rights, and supporting asylum.
3	11	Migrants increasingly traveling through Mexico via caravans, including families and unaccompanied minors. INM provides humanitarian support, including increased- deployment of Child Protection Officers, albeit participating in child separation policies.
4	32	Trump's migration policies receive mixed reviews: Obrador's support of Trump policies comes from Mexico's weaker bargaining position related to economic relations with the US. However, while no one questions Trump's right to protect US security, Trump's policies have negative repercussions on migrants (no longer reporting crimes, attending medical appointments, or registering for social programs). Some in Mexico claim Obrador should support migrants.

(Continued)

Mexico 4 Clusters		
#	%	Description of Cluster Themes
		Trump calls undocumented immigrants criminals, uses fear tactics, and leads to humanitarian issues. Religious leaders call for greater support for migrants and policy addressing the root causes of CA migration given that Mexican migration has decreased.
5	25	CA social issues prompting migration. Migrants from CA disappear on journey. Sympathy for migrants while criticizing Trump's use of migrant children as shields. Need for migration policy reform.

NT Media Narratives

NT Time Period 2

NT media narratives originally center on transnational organizations, government authorities, and civil society as the primary agents as well as congressional leaders in the US and CA. The scene, or context, in which migration occurs is placed within a transnational frame as well as focusing on the poor living conditions migrants find themselves in, with calls for aid and development programs for CA countries, as well as social support for migrants. The migration journey is reported as dangerous, with migrants traveling through CA into Mexico to enter the US. Key acts include a variety of government authorities enforcing migration policies such as separating families, conducting raids on illegal migrants, and building fences or walls. These policies are characterized as controversial, even xenophobic, and aimed at stoking fear. Additional themes

NT P2

Key agents: Whole (world, organization, country); Authorities (federal, US, local); US (House, Congress, Senate, government); Guatemalans (community, migrant, foreign ministry); Latin/Central American (citizens, civil society, Congress, pan/union); people (young, live, leave)

Scene: Poor living conditions (subhuman, lacking legal rights, few resources, little attention, poor economy, conflict); Settlement locations; US politics (Democrats/Republicans don't know/ understand; sympathize); Transnational perspectives, flows; locations (Latin American, Central America, Mexico border, Caribbean, Arizona, US, south, Florida, New York, New Jersey, metropolitan, country); Journey (dangerous, unfortunate, destination, American, attempt, continue, illegally); private (school, residence, sector, space)

Acts: Enforcement (raids, wall, return home, family separation, laws, convict); Racist (public debate, political statements, controversial, xenophobic policies, places); Leave (people, country, immigrant, family, society, move abroad); Go (learn English, immigrant); conflict, family; Receive (family, society, send, approval; country); New (create, security, status, citizen, legislation, life); Ask (needs, wants, stop, migration); Exercise (right, caution).

Instrument: Legal (authorization, resident, status, service, health); Policies (migrant and trade, create, registration process, public, health); Work (visa, temporary, agricultural, permit); Aid (development, program, legal, provide, social, immigration, offer); Remittance; Asylum

Enforcement: Gigantic (fence, wall), raids (fear);

Purpose: Basic freedoms, necessities, social justice; Seek better opportunities, health, America viewed as land of opportunity, different culture; Family reunification; Better life (normalize, risk, cycle); US citizenship; health (good, public, insurance, mental, problem); economic development

include CA migrants leaving their family and countries to go learn English and emigrate to the US in pursuit of economic opportunities and a better life. The US is viewed as a land of opportunity whereby migrants may be able to escape the cycle of violence in their home nations.

Narrative clusters revolve primarily around poor conditions in migrants' country of origin coupled with economic opportunities in the US, marking migration as a transnational issue. Migrants are thus motivated to endure harassment, discrimination, and threats to life in pursuit of a better life in the US. The primary driver of migration is reported as economic, with migrants working in the US to send back remittances to support families and purchase basic necessities. The US is criticized for demonizing immigrants, criminalizing migration, and hurting migrant families; with US immigration reform emphasizing border security and temporary worker agreements.

NT 2 Clusters		
#	%	Description of Cluster Themes
0	20	Migration is not a choice but is forced upon migrants convinced their country's economic situation is unable to fulfill their legitimate aspirations to live in better conditions. Thus, migrants come to the US because of its need for low-priced labor, with families venturing across deserts and experiencing harassment to seek a better future. The US only discusses immigration during elections and carries out mass deportations and raids on workplaces, placing people in precarious legal situations.
1	22	Discussion of back and forth political negotiations among Democrats and Republicans in Congress and President Bush's White House regarding immigration reform, resulting in the bill failing to move forward. Key issues include making English the national language, temporary worker program for undocumented immigrants, and concerns over amnesty granted. Democrats and Republicans reached some agreement on establishing a merit system for obtaining residence based primarily on labor market demands followed by education, command of English, and family ties. Hispanic groups' main concern includes family reunification of immigrants inside and outside of the US.
2	18	Over 100,000 migrants returned to their country of origin amid record-setting migration expected to continue rising. Migrants travel to the US in order to send badly needed remittances to families back home to pay for food, clothing, shelter, transportation, and other basic necessities. Migrants are victims of thieves, coyotes, and police officers. Catholic Church provides migrants with food, shelter, and medicine, while other organizations monitor and protect migrants' human rights. Increased funding for immigration agents reduces organized crime and contributes to the successful apprehension and return of migrants to country of origin. New policies state migrants traveling without permission lose right to enter the US again.

3	9	Discussions on US immigration reform legislation—emphasizing border security, including more walls, agents, and security perimeters, needing to come before temporary worker agreement. Other immigration reform issues include temporary worker program that allows guests to work in US for six years, with workers returning to country of origin every two years; increased sanctions against companies hiring undocumented immigrants; and questions over efficacy of establishing English as national language. Immigrants viewed as important contributors to US economy, while US politicians exhibit resentment toward workers doing jobs in the US that no one else wants or can do, with the US failing to recognize the positive elements of immigration, highlighting only negative aspects.
4	15	Criticisms of US demonizing immigrants, discriminating against them, destroying families through deportation and raids, and criminalizing them unfairly for simply leaving their family and land in search of a better standard of living while significantly contributing to the US economy. Description of proposed US immigration reform and pathway to permanent residence permit, with head of family required to return to country of origin within eight years, pay a fine of $5,000, demonstrate command of English, and pass a criminal background check.
5	17	Discussion of the transnational nature of migration resulting from capital and labor flows centering on the implications toward Puerto Rico and the Caribbean, with migrants coming from Latin America. Human trafficking poses problems requiring public policy and intervention tools to protect children as well as migrants causing brain drain. Immigration system should be restructured to include a merit system considering educational level, skills, and command of English.

NT Time Period 3

Time Period 3 narratives continue to include government agencies and legislatures in CA and US as key agents as well as transnational organizations and civil society actors but now also include Mexican cartels and criminal organizations, activists, with a greater emphasis on migrants as young, and as including women and children. The location in which migration occurs becomes more specific, with emphasis on NT nations and Mexican territory, albeit still including the US southern border with coverage emphasizing record numbers of migrants and deportations occurring. Migrants' purpose for migrating still includes economic and family-related reasons, including working in the US and sending back remittances as well, as more broadly, seeking a better life. More emphasis, however, is placed on migrants' desire for human rights, dignity, security, and respect; especially as news media report migrants experiencing human rights violations and falling victim to human trafficking. Enforcement actions are still prevalently mentioned, such as deportations, but more discussion turns to supporting reform of immigration laws and policies.

NT P3

Key agents: Government (Guatemalan, Mexican, federal, authority, police, executive, legislative, president, Central America, Latin America, Puerto Rico, official, country); US (Obama, Congress, federal); People (young, undocumented); Population (Puerto Rican, immigrant/migrant); Mexican cartels; Organization (migrant, criminal, civil rights, Hispanic, international, community, nongovernmental, UN, INM); Family (women, young, immigrant, pregnant, child); Community (immigrant, migrant, Hispanic, Latino); National (council, institute, coalition, registry, civil, center, association, directorate, institute, commission, advisory, secretary, legislative); activists; Ministry (Foreign, Public)

Scene: Locations (Central America, Latin, SA, Mexican territory, Guatemala, Honduras, El Salvador, US, country, metropolitan/rural/urban); borders (south, Mexico, north, Arizona, Texas, New York); record increases of (immigrant, undocumented, deport, year, case, economic situation; numbers, deportation, deportee); living conditions

Acts: Human rights violations; human trafficking; Family (remittance, separate); Work; travel, reach, try, enter, deport, cross (US, illegally, Mexico); leave (country, people); border crossing, increase; country (leave, enter, illegally, return, receive, live); Deport (immigrant, Guatemalans, people, more, migrant, immigration); reside, reform; know better; crime (organized, commit)

Instrument: Civil rights; Remittance; Enforcement (state, law, police, authorities, law, policy); Commissions (migrant, rights, legislative, human, president, national); Travel (alone, illegally, minor, train, trafficking); temporary work permits, visas; deportation; policy (immigration, new, law, measure)

Purpose: Human rights, dignity, security, respect, stop crime and rights violations; Support family; Secure, control, strengthen border; Work together; Support (immigration, reform, migrant, comprehensive, Obama); Find way (different, better); opportunity (better, job, employment); economic development

Narrative clusters revolve around CA migrants caught in the US legal system where they suffer from inhumane treatment and are left vulnerable and scared. CA migrants are reported as leaving their country of origin and traveling to the US out of a desire for dignity and a better life. CA migrants are discussed as remaining committed to traveling to the US despite harsh treatment and victimization during the journey and at the hands of US migration authorities in particular. US migration authorities and its legal system are reported as overwhelmed by the flow of migration, lacking the resources to humanely manage migrants and migrant families and adjudicate their cases in a timely manner. As coverage of these abuses are reported, NT media increasingly picks up on civil society groups challenging US migration policies.

NT 3 Clusters		
#	%	Description of Cluster Themes
0	24	Mexican and CA migrants caught in US legal system, with courts litigating parts of US immigration law. While awaiting deportation and legal process, migrants are left vulnerable, scared, with little food, clothes, diapers, and supplies. Focus on female migrants, with heartbreaking scenes of migrants anxiously awaiting processing at overcrowded Greyhound bus stops.

(*Continued*)

NT 3 Clusters		
#	%	Description of Cluster Themes
1	17	Civil society and religious groups calling into question legal issues associated with Obama administration's immigration laws as well as and treatment of migrants from Guatemalan officials. Civil society groups suing US government on illegally detaining people by their immigration status. Treatment of young migrant man by Guatemalan officials resulted in his death, with calls for investigation. Pope Francis calls for countries to facilitate movement of immigrants and avoid trafficking.
2	24	Hundreds of undocumented CA immigrants being arrested in Arizona and Texas, with ICE and US Border Patrol overwhelmed and lacking resources to detain and deport the large number of migrants, especially families with children. Lack of resources and preparation, including limited number of border patrol agents, causing US officials to doubt the efficacy of US immigration strategy. Migrants have 15 days to handle their cases, with ICE putting migrants on return flights. Migrants treated inhumanely, causing them to get sick and die.
3 & 4	21	A movie depicting teenage immigrant travelers on a train to the US won nine awards at the 56th Ariel Awards for Mexican cinema. The movie highlights the sadness and suffering of many migrants while celebrating Mexican pride. The movie tells the story of people who are looking for a dream and along the way encounter the cruelty of those who want to extort, violate, or even kill them. The characters in the movie start from the lowest positions in society, make indescribable sacrifices, and eventually reach positions of respect and productivity unobtainable if they stayed home. The movie calls for reflection and understanding for what it means to migrate and change places where one lives and works. The production team dedicated the film to immigrants and ask authorities to improve migrant conditions.

NT 3 Clusters		
#	%	Description of Cluster Themes
5	14	CA migrate out of desire for dignity and value for life. Despite dangers and little success rate, young people are determined to migrate. CA face the problem of young unemployment, which demoralizes and alienates them from society. Migrants are victims of globalization and indifference, with their situation exposing them to dangers such as human trafficking, forced labor, and slavery. However, CA should reflect on what they lose from migration, specifically their relations with friends and family and not only search for material benefit provided by migration.

NT Time Period 4

Time Period 4 narratives list similar agents as Time Period 3 (government agencies, migrant children, families, minors; civil society actors, US congressional leaders) but now also focus on US President Donald Trump and the National Guard. The context of migration remains largely the same, with record increases in migration cases from NT nations and migration occurring primarily along the US southern border. However, description of migrants' journey is less prevalent, with migration characterized as irregular. Migrants' motivations remain reported as economic and as seeking out a better life. News coverage includes migrants repeatedly attempting to enter the US, but now also adds considerable discussion of asylum and further calls for protecting migrants' human rights, dignity, and security. Actions still include human trafficking, deportation, detention, and family separation, with further calls for civil society actors and government agencies to advocate, defend, and protect migrants as well as securing their right to due process.

NT P4

Key agents: Government (Guatemalan, Mexican, Honduran, El Salvadoran, American, federal, local, authority, Central American); Group (criminal, migrant, people, family); Migrants (Guatemalan, women, Mexican, child, Honduran, Salvadoran, caravan, Central American); Young people (child, parent, family, adolescent, women, immigrant, minor); President (American, Trump, Obama, Sanchez, Guatemalan, Lopez, Lopez, Biden, Salvadoran, Obrador, Honduran); US/America (president, government, authority, official, Trump, Secretary, Congress, Caribbean); Organizations associated with migration (national, directorate, international, Guatemalan, IOM, director, ACLU, civil society, INM); National (guard, police, council, registry, agent); Northern Triangle

Scene: Record increases in migration, cases, child, people, undocumented, family; Territory/border (Guatemalan, Mexican; Southern border—US, Mexico, Chiapas, California, Central America, triangle); Situation (irregular, economic, immigration, difficult, political, social, structural, vulnerable, legal, experience); Migratory flow (leave, enter, return, come, cross, seek, reach arrive, origin country); crisis (humanitarian, migration, order, economic, political, refugee)

Acts: Human trafficking; migrants' rights (violated, abuse, dignity, respect); Family (reunification, separation, remittance, child, migrant); Minor/child (travel, arrive, separate, deport, detain); Enter, cross, reach, try, stop, travel, return (migrant, child, family, asylum, voluntarily, forcibly), arrive, come, leave (southern border, Mexico, US, illegally, alone, minor, irregular, caravan); Leave (Honduras, Salvador, Honduras, Guatemala, country, people, young); Deport (Guatemalans); detain (migrant, immigrant, child, undocumented); Ask (Trump, US, Congress, government).

Instrument: Caravans; US (policy, law, citizenship); Receive (asylum, remittance); Unaccompanied; civil society (advocate, defend, protect—migrants); Due process; Policy (immigration, tolerance, anti-immigration/immigrant, separation, family, border, President Donald Trump, America/US); national cooperation/agreements/meetings (sign, Guatemala, trade, US, Mexico, Guatemala, bilateral); deportation

Purpose: American Dream; asylum; human (dignity, security, respect); rights (human, migrant, defender, respect, guarantee, protect, advocate); Life (better, improve, save, quality, risk, dignified, lose, decent); migrants take (advantage, action, refuge, child); national security; generate/promote economic and social development/opportunity; stop (illegal/irregular migration, poverty); escape/flee violence and gangs

Narrative clusters revolve around discussion of its structural causes, in contrast to the Trump administration's hardened migration policies. NT media reports that Trump's policies lead only to more migration and more dangerous paths, with coverage of the Trump administration's hardened anti-migration policies viewed as criminalizing migration, which results in inhumane treatment of migrants and is judged illegal both by US courts and the American Civil Liberties Union (ACLU). Narrative clusters also include discussion of migration's root causes, specifically economic issues—including poverty and unemployment— as well as misery in the home nation, again described as leaving to pursue a better life. As such, migration is reported as a transnational issue requiring multinational cooperation in partnership with civil society partners, both in combating inhumane treatment of migrants during their journey and in promoting economic and social policies mitigating the desire for migration. In contrast to the US, Mexico is reported as preparing for CA migrants by setting up refuge stations, with migrants reporting as stopping in Mexico to begin their process of applying for humanitarian visas in the US.

NT 4 Clusters		
#	%	Description of Cluster Themes
0	9	Reports of Mexican authorities intercepting migrants and criminals traveling to US. Migrants from CA are attacked by gunman; others are kidnapped by traffickers or disappeared. Migrants include young men, women, and children. Associated with the arrests are dangerous criminals.
1	29	Multinational cooperative elements with civil society partners to address migration and dangers associated with it. Government cooperation combating crime related to human trafficking, smuggling, and protection of safety of migrants; and ensuring humanitarian assistance for migrants. Migration caused by structural elements, including poverty, unemployment, fear, and misery in home country—in sum, search for a better life. On migration routes, migrants are victims of kidnapping, extortion, organized crime, and human trafficking. Problem requires a shared responsibility by countries involved.

(Continued)

NT 4 Clusters		
#	%	Description of Cluster Themes
2	10	CA governments working on policies to mitigate migration by addressing its structural causes with the aim of reducing poverty as well as seeking funds to strengthen police and military institutions. El Salvador actively promoting economic and social policies as part of multinational Plan of the Alliance for Prosperity to reduce migration and generating opportunities and well-being for the regional population. Criticisms of Trump and Pence's rhetoric, specifically Trump's tough immigration policies sparking migrant communities to migrate, including use of coyotes. Trump criticizes CA governments for failing to control migration and threatens to withdraw aid.
3	28	Trump's pursuit of zero-tolerance policies against migrants criminalizing migration and separating thousands of migrant children from their families. ACLU and US judges rule against Trump's child separation policy, with Trump's policies illegal, inhumane, and part of his reelection strategy.
4	17	CA migrant caravans entering Mexico, hoping to enter the US by requesting asylum. Mexican authorities preparing for the large influx of CA migrants by setting up refuge stations and creating special humanitarian visa allowing CA migrants to enter and work in Mexico. Most CA migrants seek to regularize their stay in Mexico with a humanitarian visa as a first step toward migrating to the US.
5	7	President Trump ordering massive raids against migration in the US carried out by ICE. Multiple raids and arrests made by ICE, with Trump portending more to come. Multiple instances of migrants with criminal backgrounds arrested and deported by US authorities. US authorities also separating thousands of minors.

US Media Narratives

US Time Period 1

US media narratives originally centered on the economic dimensions of Mexican migration. Mexican migrants are the primary actors described as day laborers and guest workers as well as undocumented and illegal immigrants. Mexican migrants' purpose for coming to the US is for work to support their families at home while also seeking US residency to obtain a better life. The scene predominantly includes increases in migration to the US and depictions of the migration journey as perilous as Mexican migrants traverse harsh terrain, often dying along the way.

US P1

Key agents: Mexicans (broadly, immigrant, worker, official, government, state) and immigrants, guest workers, undocumented, illegal, migrant, day laborers, men, population (immigrant, Hispanic); Governments (US, Mexico, country, state, federal, official, State Department, Secretary of State Colin); US and Mexican presidents (Bush and Clinton administration); residents (permanent, legal, long time; border patrol agents); UN

Scene: Journey (desert, towns, dying, border crossing); increases in migration (residents, workers, people, immigrants); places (Mexico, Arizona, California, Central/South/Latin/North America); economic use of migrants (day laborers); migrants living in the shadows; uneducated/unskilled migrant workers; birth rate

Acts: granting (legalization, amnesty); work (getting money, jobs, visas, immigrant); illegal immigration (flow, crossing, increasing); dying

Instrument: guest worker program/permits; punishment; create jobs; migration reform policies; water stations.

Purpose: better life, work, residency, economic (growth, development, opportunity); stop drug trafficking

Narrative clusters revolve around US–Mexican bilateral relationship. Economic conditions are reported as the drivers of migration, with Mexican immigrants performing low-skilled jobs in the US in inhumane conditions. Coverage includes Congressional Republicans and Democrats as unable to come to agreement on immigration reform with guest worker programs taking center stage but with a path to legalization decried as amnesty. Increasing anti-immigrant rhetoric comes from US workers and Republicans worried about Mexican immigrants taking US jobs, and border security initiatives only push migrants to take more dangerous routes to the US, resulting in more migrant deaths.

US 1 Clusters		
#	%	Description of Cluster Themes
0	8	The Californian border has transformed from an easy access point under siege from illegal immigration to virtually no immigration due to the installation of lights and ground sensors, fencing, and doubling the number of border patrol agents. However, this has only pushed illegal immigrants to more dangerous terrain, such as remote mountains and deserts, with many dying from exposure to extreme heat or cold, sparking criticism from human rights groups.
1	12	Political infighting and hypocrisy surrounding President Bush's incipient immigration reform bill that would focus on creating a guest worker program and a path to citizenship for 3–4 million immigrants. Criticism centers on amnesty, although this amnesty shootout is increasingly disconnected from the substance of the issue. Both Democrats and Republicans are viewed as opposing amnesty, noting that amnesty doesn't sell; nonetheless, Democrats once supported a similar plan proposed by Bush during the Clinton administration, but now oppose Bush's plan. Republicans also remain skeptical of Bush's plan, while Bush is viewed as courting Latinos, a crucial voting bloc for Bush.
2	31	Immigration reform efforts focusing on penalizing businesses that hire undocumented workers. Typical immigration policies, such as securing the border, have proved ineffectual, prompting a new strategy to make life in the US unattractive for immigrants by closing down the job market and penalizing employers. Immigrants come to the US for economic reasons despite being exploited in the US and forced to work in inhumane conditions.
3	21	Despite a weakening US economy, Mexico's even poorer economic circumstances prompting Mexican immigration to the US. US workers and unions are opposed to Mexican immigration, fearing new proposed guest worker programs will bring in more Mexicans, taking US jobs from US workers. Anti-immigrant rhetoric is increasing over concerns regarding jobs. Mexican immigrants living in California face poor school conditions. Mexican immigrants are forced to come to the US for the promise of US jobs.

| 4 | 11 | Anti-immigrant sentiment threatening political cooperation on immigration reform. President Bush is characterized as differing from Republicans through his support for immigration. Republicans chastised for their rhetoric of compassion being at odds with their harsh anti-immigrant agenda. Discussion centers around political jockeying for Hispanic votes with historical discussions of Reagan's policies, Hispanics' culturally conservative nature, and Democrats' generally pro-immigration sentiment and support of the White House on immigration reform. |
| 5 | 16 | President Bush and Fox meet to discuss US–Mexico relations, specifically immigration. The two leaders are described as cooperative in negotiating key issues such as immigration, drug trafficking, and energy, with President Fox taking the initiative to place immigration at the center of the bilateral relationship. |

US Time Period 2

Time Period 2 contains similar narratives focusing on Mexican migrants coming to the US for economic purposes—seeking out low-skilled jobs such as construction to earn money to send home to support their families; however, migrant families and their children are also now mentioned. Additional agents include US and Mexican government authorities taking steps to enforce immigration laws, including arrests, detention, and deportation of illegal migrants. Nonetheless, migrants are reported as circumventing these prevention efforts by finding new routes, often more dangerous, and using smuggling rings to help them cross the border. Additionally, coverage includes concerns of Mexican migrants as taking US jobs and taking advantage of the US system, as well as seeking out the American Dream.

US P2

Key agents: Mexican workers (undocumented, illegal, migrant); day laborers; smugglers; Government (US, Mexico, federal, local, agents-border patrol, customs, authorities, state); population (immigrant, Hispanic, growth, illegal, undocumented); University (California State, professor); Latin/Central/South America; National Guard (troops)

Scene: Increases (migrants, workers, smuggling); US (coming, north, working in, border, enter, live, year); US–Mexico Border; Landscape of crossing (deserts, rivers, rural, Mexico, into US); places (California, North Carolina, Texas, Arizona, New Mexico); home (country, send, return, money, state, immigrant)

Acts: New (immigrant, create, law, program, system; rule; arrival); Jobs (hiring of undocumented, worker, immigrant, lose, create, work permit); Crossing border, entering US, dying; Smuggling (immigrants, drugs, coyote, gangs); Home (send, return, go back, send money); Enforcement (arrest, detain, failure, program, deportation, catch, Border patrol, illegal, fence); leave child; come (forward, home, illegal, migrant, family, country, immigrant, worker); live (immigrant, US, Salvadoran, illegally, family); bring

Instrument: Circumventing (smuggling rings, boats, new routes, chain migration); Prevention (border patrol, enforcement, fence); Programs (guest worker, new, immigrant, create); Family support (money, send home, transfer, raise); policy (INM); work (visa, permit, temporary); fence (border, build, wall)

Purpose: Support family (remittances/money); Work (low skilled, wages, construction, seek, obtain); American Dream; US citizenship, legal residence; US jobs, take advantage, create, lose; slow/stop illegal immigrant flow; economic development

Narrative clusters revolve around US policies aiming to strengthen border security and tighten guest worker programs. Thus, the causes of migration are reported as economic, with Mexican immigrants pursuing creative, alternative means to bypass increases to US border security such as smugglers and underground tunnels. Other themes include reports explaining Congressional Republicans' focus on border security, in contrast to President Bush and Democrats' focus on guest worker programs. Domestically, US workers are concerned with Mexican immigrants taking US jobs and squeezing wages.

US 2 Clusters		
#	%	Description of Cluster Themes
0	24	Debate over US immigration bill that would criminalize immigration rather than its current status as a civil violation. Primary concerns are with economic issues, including providing immigrants with a guest worker program and identification cards. Mexico's stagnant economy cited as reason for immigration. Republican representatives criticizing President Bush's immigration reform bill wanting to focus on controlling US borders.
1	17	President Bush's push for immigration reform faces fierce opposition from conservative leaders. Republicans increasingly campaigning on anti-immigrant positions, focusing on border security. President Bush and Senate Democrats on the same page regarding guest worker programs. President Bush emphasizing investments in border security to win over Republicans. Republicans' lack of action on immigration contributing to their loss of the House and Senate majorities, while Democrats face pressure from their political base to take action on immigration reform.
2	2	US politics polarized over immigration reform, with headlines from letters to the editor representing positions in favor and against immigration reform. Washington viewed as being in a state of paralysis. Congressional Republicans criticized for irrationally dealing with migration, suggesting they follow President Bush's lead; especially as Hispanics appear largely in favor of Bush's policies.
3	28	Coverage reporting on the effects of immigrants onto the labor market. Illegal immigration drives down wages, with guest worker programs furthering wage squeeze. Labor-intensive, low-skill jobs attract foreign workers from Mexico and Latin America, specifically in farming, cleaning, and construction. Immigrants are less likely to be unionized.

(Continued)

US 2 Clusters		
#	%	Description of Cluster Themes
4	11	US is significantly stiffening security on the US–Mexico border, making migration more difficult but not stopping it from increasing. Smugglers are forced to adapt and become more creative with their smuggling attempts, even going underground through tunnels. Smugglers charging a higher price for their services due to increased security. Continued strengthening of the border unlikely to reduce the surge of illegal immigration, although some reports claim additional fencing and manpower provide powerful deterrents.
5	19	Illegal Mexican immigrants in the US are able to send money back home through new remittance programs put in place by US financial system. Economic development fuels Mexican migration, with a poor Mexican economy likely to increase immigration. Mexicans prefer immigrating to the US to seek better job opportunities. US immigration system criticized for being xenophobic, immoral, and stupid, while also noting concerns regarding illegal Mexican immigrants being able to draw upon Social Security through fraudulent Social Security identification numbers when working in the US and Mexican immigrants preferring to stay in the US to work rather than returning home.

US Time Period 3

Time Period 3 narratives shift considerably from past narratives, now including discussion of not only Mexican migrants but also CA migrants, as well as young people more generally. The motivation for migration still includes finding work, including remittances to send home to support migrant families, with discussion on migrants having to leave their families and children. However, additional goals of securing human rights and basic human dignity arise in US coverage with US goals of border security emerging prominently as well. The scene of migration still focuses on the perils of the journey, with migrants dying on the way, with focus turning to Arizona and Texas as the key entry points as illegal immigrants consistently try and re-try to illegally enter the US. US and Mexican authorities are still mentioned as engaging in a variety of enforcement actions and searching out additional instruments to prevent migration, such as border fencing and increased deportation. However, illegal immigrants are reported as increasingly turning to smugglers, drug cartels, and human trafficking, which results in additional abuses during the journey, including kidnapping and death.

US P3

Key agents: Mexican (immigrant, authority, government, migrant, workers); Central American (migrants, leaders, immigrants); Authorities (US and Mexican immigration, federal, agents, officials); Young people; Drug cartel; research/experts (Pew); University of California; State Department; Latin America

Scene: Mexican borders (north and south); Increasing (population, people, illegal, immigrant, border security) Central and Latin American); US southern border, Arizona, Texas; Difficult journey (desert, border towns Drug war, smuggle); US economy; home (country, return, send)

Acts: Human trafficking, abuses; Crossing (entering US, border, try and again, journey north, illegal); Enforcement (agents apprehend, catch few, arrest, border agency); Home (return, back, send, money, call); Deaths, kidnapping (migrants); Work (hard, legally); Family (leaving, bringing, children); explore (daily); come (US, people, immigrant, forward); live (immigrant, people, illegally, US)

Instrument: Smuggling (human trafficking, hire); Enforcement (border fence, deportation, agency, law); Guest worker program; Shelters (homeless, migrant, temporary); Remittances; Farm Work; Taking jobs; new immigration law; political asylum

Purpose: Human rights, dignity; border security, enforcement, control; US citizenship; Find (study, work, take jobs); political asylum

Narrative clusters revolve around US politicians negotiating immigration reform within the context of a larger, broken immigration system that treats immigrants unfairly, especially once they are in the US. Media report criticisms of US immigration policies as including long wait periods for processing immigration claims, use of detention facilities, and unfair treatment of children and unaccompanied minors. Although reports express the US DACA program as providing some work opportunities and reprieves from deportation, with the Obama administration focusing on deporting immigrants with criminal backgrounds, Republican support for further legislation is reported as lacking, with claims of needing to secure US borders first. Finally, an additional narrative includes how immigrants assimilate into US culture once in the US, with coverage emphasizing that immigrants come to work honorably and are assimilating into US culture but that more progress needs to be made in this area.

US 3 Clusters		
#	%	Description of Cluster Themes
0	15	Discussions on the historical population implications of Mexican migration to the US. Mexican migration from the 1970s onward has contributed to significant population growth in California. However, recently, Mexican migration has declined due to beefed-up border security coupled with fewer job prospects in the US.
1	12	Discussion of the Supreme Court battle over the Obama administration's challenging of Arizona laws related to immigration. The Obama administration alleges that Arizona's law violates the federal government's right to enforce immigration law. President Obama's policy focuses on deporting immigrants convicted of serious crimes. US immigration policy, more broadly, is described as unfair, specifically toward immigrant children and unaccompanied minors.
2	35	US immigration policy described as broken, with immigrants waiting over ten years before their applications are processed. However, positive descriptions of the Obama administration's DACA program, allowing some immigrants to obtain work permits and reprieves from deportation, although not conferring lawful immigration status. Immigrants claim that some in the US view immigrants as a plague, despite immigrants coming here to work honorably. Immigrant groups are assimilating into US society, with younger immigrants learning English, obtaining higher levels of education, and climbing the socio-economic ladder; but more progress is argued to be needed. Evangelical groups advocate for immigration overhaul on the basis of family unity, human dignity, border security, and fairness to taxpayers.

3	19	Largely optimistic portrayals of Congressional Democrats and Republicans negotiating a new immigration reform bill. Emphasis is placed on new measures to secure the border, including funds for more border agents, fencing, and aerial surveillance. Democrats primary priorities include a pathway for citizenship, while Republican support is more difficult to obtain, stressing the need for a secure border first.
4	4	Criticism over immigrant detention facilities, specifically privately run facilities. Despite record low immigration from Mexico, the number of detained immigrants remains high in private facilities due to a requirement by Congress that ICE fills a daily quota of more than 30,000 beds. Detaining immigrants, especially in private detention facilities, criticized as costing taxpayers. Immigrant labor is exploited in the detention centers where immigrants are paid 13 cents an hour. Immigrants held in detention facilities conducting hunger strikes to demand better conditions and an end to deportations.
5	15	Mexican migration is down to its lowest levels since the 1980s–1990s, with some evidence of Mexican immigrants returning to Mexico. The primary cause is economic, with fewer job opportunities in the US. Nonetheless, CA migration represents a larger than ever share of illegal border crossings. Despite funding for more fencing and border agents and lower levels of illegal immigration, apprehensions of illegal migrants are on the rise.

US Time Period 4

Time Period 4 narratives continue to shift away from Mexican migrants simply coming to the US for low-wage jobs to description of a crisis on the border whereby CA migrants attempt to escape violence and poverty at home while facing significant abuse on their journey through Mexico to the US. US and Mexican government authorities continue to be frequently mentioned as engaging in a variety of enforcement efforts, with additional description of family separation policies and detention facilities. US goals remain securing the border while increasing influxes of CA migrants traveling in caravans to the US and applying for asylum overwhelm the US immigration system and immigration courts. Accordingly, reports note how this large influx and lack of capacity force migrants to wait long periods of time before their cases are heard. During this time period, advocacy groups become prominently mentioned agents standing up for migrant rights.

US P4: Narrative Components within TOP 75 POS (KWIC)

Key agents: Central American (migrants, family, children, caravan); Presidents (Trump, Obama, Bush, Pence, new administration); People (young, many, more, American, undocumented), parents; Group (advocacy, large, rights, immigrant, nonprofit); US and Mexican government authorities/agents (border patrol, ICE, immigration, federal, enforcement, customs); Homeland (security, department, official, secretary); Courts (immigration, federal); Guatemala; refugee; political (issue, party, Trump)

Scene: Border crisis (more migrant, immigrant, child, families; thousands of people, record numbers, surge, increase border enforcement and arrest); Journey (more difficult, illegal entry); Central/Latin America (violence, poverty, children, fleeing, asylum, leave—Honduras, Guatemala, Nicaragua, El Salvador, Mexico); US/Mexican border; north (head, travel, migrant)

Acts: Caravans (arrival, large, head, travel, chain migration); Illegally cross, enter, here, come, live, begin, leave, reach US; try (cross, enter); Travel (leaving country, migrants, family, child, home; alone, group, border, country, Mexico, north); Asylum (claim, seek, apply, request, deny; wait (asylum seeker, month, period, outside, US)); Parent/child/family (separate, detain, deport, undocumented, immigrant, reunite, unaccompanied, flee); Home (return, back, leave, stay, come, violence, child, go, flee, send money); Enforcement (arrests, detention—family, child, federal, ICE, hold, expand, camps), separation, apprehend, catch, custody; Courts (hearing, ruling, decision, block, await); violence and poverty (flee)

Instrument: Enforcement (border wall, new policy, rule; child separation, detain, take, detention centers/facilities, deportation courts/asylum cases, arrest, shooting); Asylum law, claims; Caravans; Shelters (child, temporary, run, government, provide); Sanctuary Cities; work (permit, visa, temporary); tariff (impose, threat, Mexico, Trump, escalate, new, percent); threat (tariff, Trump, security, pose, national, death, safety); new (administration, policy, rule, border, wall, arrival, facility, program); trade deal/agreement; visa program

Purpose: Border/national security, protection; Asylum, refuge, protection, family; Escaping violence, poverty, humanitarian crisis; Take jobs/advantage (immigrants); economic growth (development, opportunity); address illegal border crossings; human rights; help (immigrant, migrant, people, Trump, Mexico, family)

Narrative clusters center on President Trump's policies to deter migration, while economic conditions are described as being the main driver of increasing migration flows from CA through Mexico, with immigrants now living in the US with little hope of achieving legal status. As a result, slow court hearings and reports of the broken immigration system are described as leading migrants to put down roots in the US. Although migrants are reported as benefiting the US economy, concerns are raised over their drain on US resources. Additional narrative themes include Trump's cracking down on illegal immigration with raids, arrests, detention, and deportation of migrants that spark legal and humanitarian criticism within the US, with migrants noted as receiving little protection while in US detention facilities and when living in the US.

US 4 Clusters		
#	%	Description of Cluster Themes
0	9	Large influx of migrants in the Rio Grande Valley overwhelming Customs and Border Protection agency. Border Patrol lacks facilities to detain everyone, leading to overcrowding and migrants held in poor conditions, outraging immigrant advocates and democratic lawmakers. Treatment of migrant children and infants criticized, leading to a humanitarian crisis, straining the agency's resources and leading to a crisis on the border.

(Continued)

US 4 Clusters		
#	%	Description of Cluster Themes
1	46	Immigrants provide economic benefits to the US economy, but new crackdowns on immigration leaves them to stay in the US. Famers rely on undocumented immigrants, and supply side demands cause immigration. However, immigrants are now living, working, and having families in the US, with little hope of achieving legal status while also denied education, health care, and public services. Concerns raised over immigrants as drain on US resources.
2	13	Mexico taking considerable steps to prevent CA migration to the US as a result of President Trump's threat to place economic tariffs on Mexico. Large numbers of migrants, including caravans, are stopped and detained by Mexican troops.
3	10	President Trump ordering ramped up immigration enforcement in multiple US cities described as a centerpiece of his promise to crack down on illegal immigration. ICE engaged in coordinated raids arrests, detaining, and sending back large numbers of CA migrants, including families. Trump's policies characterized as ambitious, hardened measures that US attorneys and advocacy groups view as constitutional violations lacking due process. Migrants are worried about the raids, contemplating moving to more immigrant-friendly states.
4	11	The Trump administration is attempting to deter immigration by CA by limiting who can apply for asylum, while US judges and immigration advocates challenge the policies' legality, claiming it violates migrants' due process rights. CA migrants, specifically, families and children, are forced to wait in Mexico while waiting for their asylum cases to be heard. While many migrants show up for their court hearings, the White House claims they do not, with migrants disappearing before their court date and becoming permanently undocumented immigrants in the US. Court hearings are slow due to the large number of claims, with migrants often putting down roots with children, jobs, and mortgages as they wait. Mixed discussion of the effectiveness of Trump's policies, with some saying they have deterred migration, while others say they have not.

US 4 Clusters		
#	%	Description of Cluster Themes
5	11	Reports of political infighting and negotiations between Congressional Democrats, Republicans, and the White House on possible immigration reform and government spending bills. Some optimism reported, with Republicans and Democrats passing an immigration bill, especially as President Trump issues statements in support of DACA, more discussion is placed on the breakdown of negotiations. President Trump promises to delay raids if a deal is made, believing the humanitarian crisis at the border will compel Democrats to negotiate. Trump's political base maintains support for anti-immigration policy, with stricter funding for border security viewed as a requirement for any deal. Trump's bargaining viewed as fueling chaos at the border while Democrats try to limit how any funding may be spent.

Discussion

This chapter has identified the narratives present in US, Mexican, and NT media, including how they shifted or remained consistent over time. As sense-making devices, narratives serve both ontological and epistemological functions, defining how a political community understands their world, sense of self, and relations to others in addition to providing information into specific policy issues (Hinck et al., 2021; Miskimmon et al., 2014). Consumption of such media narratives provide repeating plotlines for national audiences to understand the problems, causes, and solutions they face (Carey, 2008), which implicate their policy preferences by furnishing audiences with motives for action (Burke, 1969). While political communities tend to fall back on routine behaviors in response to uncertain or threatening circumstances (Mitzen, 2006), new narratives can nonetheless emerge during times of crisis (Subotić, 2016). To determine the potential for narrative alignment, and thus the constraints and overlays of possible imagined outcomes associated with managing migration in Northern America, we situate the discussion of our findings by assessing areas of convergence and divergence among US, Mexican, and NT media descriptions of the scene, acts, agents, instruments, and purpose surrounding CA migration, including their similarities and differences regarding phenomenon of interests, casual claims, and elements of exclusion–inclusion.

First, the scene in which migration occurs appears largely undisputed across US, Mexican, and NT media, although worsening over time. Thus, the general phenomenon of interest appears shared, with all three reporting how, over the past two decades, increasing numbers of migrants are embarking on a dangerous journey to the US. In doing so, migrants traverse harsh climates and increasingly suffer from significant humanitarian abuse, violence, family separation, and loss of life. Such narratives reflect previous studies finding news media defining migration as a crisis with humanitarian consequences (Benson, 2013, Coutin & Chock 1995), with this scenic framing of migrants placing them as victims of abuse. As D'Amato and Lucarelli (2019) explain, such reporting denies migrants their subjectivity and individual agency, and demonstrates similarities across cases in how migrants are rhetorically excluded from society more broadly.

An additional scenic similarity shared in the coverage is the portrayal of migrations as a phenomenon characterized by crisis. Indeed, this crisis narrative only becomes more acute as time goes on as migrants, on reaching the US border, are similarly reported as facing a US immigration system overwhelmed, leaving migrants with little recourse, contributing to perceptions of migrants as treated in an undignified, inhumane manner. Nonetheless, while all three nations portray migration as a crisis with migrants victimized throughout the process, a key scenic element missing from US considerations is discussions of its root causes: migrants' escaping poverty and violence experienced within their country of origin. Here, the casual claims appear to diverge as NT media most frequently report on the dire conditions migrants face at home, with such explanations also prevalent in Mexican media as well. While this gap in US reporting may be reflective of what Boswell and Badenhoop (2019) call "state ignorance," or the lacking of knowledge relevant to addressing social problems, US authorities are reported as responding not with denial or resignation but greater efforts to fund and secure the US southern border.

Second, and like the scenic elements of migration, the actions most frequently covered by all three media systems converge, showing a similar phenomenon of interests across cases through their reporting of migrants as leaving their homes to travel to the US, which leads to their detention, deportation, separation of family, and acts of violence committed against them. Unfortunately, however, these reported acts dominate the narratives on migration, which, in turn, results in discussions within the US, but also Mexico, focusing on deterrent actions and enforcement mechanisms, thereby leading to US media narratives, in particular, to draw different causal inferences about how to stem the causes of migration. The consequence of this action-oriented focus is the bringing of attention to the immediate situation in which migration is being reported, accentuating a narrative of crisis focusing on the increase in migrants, the inability to process their large number at the US border, and the abuses migrants face not at home but on their migratory journey. This narrative structure falls into what Steinhilper and Gruijters (2018) call deterrence-oriented narratives, where states, devoid of systematic information on the drivers of migration, pursue stricter border controls but fail to address humanitarian concerns. In other words, US—and to a lesser extent—Mexican narratives place the scene of action not within NT nations but on the route to the US, obscuring the deeper drivers of irregular migration, and marks one of the largest divergences between US and NT media narratives.

Third, and following the action-oriented narrative of migration, key agents mentioned from all three media systems include government agencies, including various US and Mexican immigration officials charged with implementing deportation-related policies. Mexican media report at length how it is enforcing migration laws through the arrests and deportations of CA migrants, which increase over time as the agents of migration shift from Mexicans to Central Americans. However, a key change in agents, shared by all three media systems, is the emergence of criminal organizations, specifically drug cartels, who financially profit and monopolize the routes through Mexico to the US, as well as illegal entry into US territory. These criminal agents prove particularly worrisome for Mexican and US society, with the former concerned with the destabilizing effects of crime associated with migration—not necessarily migrants themselves but the empowerment of criminal organizations and their corrupting influence on Mexican politics as migrants increasingly rely on them to circumvent US border protections. Such dynamics may contribute to concerns linking migrants with criminality and illegality (Jones-Correa & de Graauw, 2013; Suro, 2008) both in the US and in Mexico. Other shifts in agents include the demographics of migrants themselves, from single, largely male, Mexican laborers to Central American families, specifically, women and children, while US mentality regarding the changing nature of those migrating remains slow to shift, viewing migrants as those simply seeking labor, or stealing jobs, leading to poorly adapted policies.

Fourth, the largest divergence appears to be on the understanding of the purposes of migrants coming to the US and the instruments or means by which they do so. Here again, we see important schisms within the data set relating to both the phenomenon of migration and the subsequent casual claims by which the US views policy options to mitigate it, thereby constraining the overlays of possible policy actions. Here, US discourse on migration increasingly solidifies into a discussion on border security, while NT and Mexican discourses emphasize migrants' humanitarian needs to seek out a better life, including economic opportunity, as well as lives free from overt violence. Thus, whereas in the first two time periods examined, US politicians more openly discussed policies, or instruments, regarding temporary work visas and paths to legalization, such discussions dissipated over time and crystalized into arguments decrying amnesty and supporting enforcement mechanisms criminalizing migration, coalescing on a single-minded focus on border security. This policy narrative reflects what Burke (1984) calls "trained incapacities," whereby US obsession with border security prevents it from adapting its responses to the changing circumstances of migration and seeking alternative modalities to reduce it.

Finally, while the right to protect one's border finds some resonance within Mexican and NT perspectives on migration, the US' preoccupation with border security is seen as inappropriately criminalizing migration while ignoring migrant's plight and empowering criminal organizations. Here, NT and Mexican media highlight the new instruments with which migrants circumvent increased US border protections through criminal organizations. Thus, a common plotline is that US border enforcement policies work only to push migrants into increasingly dangerous illegal pathways to reach the US, contributing to migrants' victimization and highlighting the failure. US narratives then largely ignore the purpose of migration consistently described within Mexican and NT media, namely, that of escaping the cycle of violence and poverty within migrants' countries of origin. Whereas NT media, in particular, highlight instruments such as the need for investment and aid to improve conditions within the NT or shelters and humanitarian aid for migrants during their journey, US narratives focusing solely on policy instruments to strengthen their own border ignore such claims, fail to address the root causes and purpose of CA migration, thereby demonstrating further divergences in the causal claims by which migration is understood and prevented. Such divergences further fuel dynamics of exclusion as US reporting ignores elements of commonality—that is, the inclusion of consideration of migrant rights as human rights more broadly. As long as such focus remains on walling off migration, rather than stemming its cause rooted in well-being, a transnational narrative of cooperation will remain difficult to imagine, let alone achieve.

REFERENCES

Benson, R. (2013). *Shaping immigration news*. Cambridge: Cambridge University Press.

Boswell, C., & Badenhoop, E. (2019). "What isn't in the files, isn't in the world": Understanding state ignorance of irregular migration in Germany and the United Kingdom. *Governance*.

Burke, K. (1969). *A grammar of motives*. University of California Press.

Burke, K. (1984). *Permanence and change: An anatomy of purpose*. University of California Press.

Carey, J. W. (2008). *Communication as culture, revised edition: Essays on media and society*. Routledge.

Cash, J., & Kinnvall, C. (2017). Postcolonial bordering and ontological insecurities. *Postcolonial Studies, 20*(3), 267–274. https://doi.org/10.1080/136887 90.2017.1391670

Castells, M. (2008). The new public sphere: Global civil society, communication networks, and global governance. *The Annals of the American Academy of Political and Social Science, 616*(1), 78–93. https://doi. org/10.1177/0002716207311877

Cooley, S., Hinck, R., & Sample, E. (2022). Northern triangle and Mexican news media perspectives on the migration crisis: strategic narrative and the identification of good action. *Migration and Development, 11*(3), 291-313.

Coutin, S. B., & Chock, P. P. (1995). "Your friend, the illegal:" Definition and paradox in newspaper accounts of US immigration reform. *Identities, 2*(1-2), 123–148. https://doi.org/10.1080/1070289X.1997.9962529

Cvajner, M., & Sciortino, G. (2010). Theorizing irregular migration: the control of spatial mobility in differentiated societies. *European Journal of Social Theory, 13*(3), 389–404. https://doi.org/10.1177/1368431010371764

D'Amato, S., & Lucarelli, S. (2019). Talking migration: Narratives of migration and justice claims in the European migration system of governance. *The International Spectator, 54*(3), 1–17. https://doi.org/10.1080/03932729.2019. 1643181

Flew, T. (2020). Globalization, neo-globalization and post-globalization: The challenge of populism and the return of the national. *Global Media and Communication, 16*(1), 19–39. https://doi.org/10.1177/1742766519900329

Flew, T., Iosifidis, P., & Steemers, J. (2016). Global media and national policies: The return of the state. In *Global media and national policies* (pp. 1-15). Palgrave Macmillan

Gurevitch, M., & Blumler, J. G. (2004). State of the art of comparative political communication research. *Comparing political communication*, 325-43.

Harris, C. T., & Gruenewald, J. (2020). News media trends in the framing of immigration and crime, 1990–2013. *Social Problems, 67*(3), 452–470. https://doi.org/10.1093/socpro/spz024

Hinck, R. S., Kitsch, S. R., Cooley, A., & Cooley, S. C. (2021). *The future of global competition: ontological security narratives in Chinese, Russian, Venezuelan, and Iranian media*. Routledge.

Jones-Correa, M., & De Graauw, E. (2013). The illegality trap: The politics of immigration & the lens of illegality. *Daedalus, 142*(3), 185–198. https://doi.org/10.1162/DAED_a_00227

Kinnvall, C. (2004). Globalization and religious nationalism: Self, identity, and the search for ontological security. *Political Psychology, 25*(5), 741–767. https://doi.org/10.1111/j.1467-9221.2004.00396.x

Kinnvall, C., & Mitzen, J. (2018). Ontological security and conflict: The dynamics of crisis and the constitution of community. *Journal of International Relations and Development, 21*(4), 825–835. https://doi.org/10.1057/s41268-018-0161-1

Kruze, M. (2019, June 14). The escalator ride that changed America. *Politico.* https://www.politico.com/magazine/story/2019/06/14/donald-trump-campaign-announcement-tower-escalator-oral-history-227148/

Miskimmon, A., O'loughlin, B., & Roselle, L. (2014). *Strategic narratives: Communication power and the new world order*. Routledge.

Mitzen, J. (2006). Ontological security in world politics: State identity and the security dilemma. *European Journal of International Relations, 12*(3), 341–370. https://doi.org/10.1177/1354066106067346

Newland, K. (2019). *Global governance of international migration 2.0: What lies ahead?*. Migration Policy Institute.

Oates, S., Gurevich, O., Walker, C., Deibler, D., & Anderson, J. (2020). *Sharing a playbook?: The convergence of Russian and U.S. narratives about Joe Biden*. American Political Science Association: 2020 APSA Annual Meeting: Democracy, Difference, and Destabilization. https://preprints.apsanet.org/engage/api-gateway/apsa/assets/orp/resource/item/5f56826c11e5c800121844be/original/sharing-a-playbook-the-convergence-of-russian-and-u-s-narratives-about-joe-biden.pdf

Palau-Sampio, D. (2018). Reframing Central American migration from narrative journalism. *Journal of Communication Inquiry*, *43*(1), 93–114. https://doi.org/10.1177/0196859918806676

Proedrou, F., & Frangonikolopoulos, C. (2012). Refocusing public diplomacy: The need for strategic discursive public diplomacy. *Diplomacy & Statecraft*, *23*(4), 728–745. https://doi.org/10.1080/09592296.2012.736339

Rogers & Bailey (2020, October 31). Trump wall: How much has he actually built? *BBC*. https://www.bbc.com/news/world-us-canada-46824649

Slaven, M., & Boswell, C. (2019). Why symbolise control? Irregular migration to the UK and symbolic policy-making in the 1960s. *Journal of Ethnic and Migration Studies*, *45*(9), 1477–1495. https://doi.org/10.1080/1369183X.2018.1459522

Steinhilper, E., & Gruijters, R. J. (2018). A contested crisis: Policy narratives and empirical evidence on border deaths in the Mediterranean. *Sociology*, *52*(3), 515–533. https://doi.org/10.1177/0038038518759248

Subotić, J. (2016). Narrative, ontological security, and foreign policy change. *Foreign Policy Analysis*, *12*(4), 610–627. https://doi.org/10.1111/fpa.12089

Suro, R. (2008). *The triumph of no: How the media influence the immigration debate*. Brookings Institution. https://www.brookings.edu/wp-content/uploads/2012/04/0925_immigration_dionne.pdf

Time. (2015, June 16). *Here's Donald Trump's presidential announcement speech*. https://time.com/3923128/donald-trump-announcement-speech/

CHAPTER 5

Triangulating News Media

Today's globalized world has brought individuals, civil society actors, and governments closer than ever before, resulting in a globally networked society facilitated by communication (Castells, 2008, 2009). While mass media plays an essential role in defining how communities understand their world, analysis of news reporting requires frameworks that capture multilevel environments among actors, news reports, and policy makers from the local to global and back (Gilboa et al., 2016). Nowhere is this more true than in discussions of migration in CA and the US.

As Harris and Gruenewald (2020) note, a growing body of sociological and political science research finds public and political discourse disconnected from empirical evidence when it comes to immigration policy. Indeed, studies show news media as generally framing migrants in a negative light by depicting them as threats to society while making claims linking them to increased violence despite empirical evidence to the contrary (Farris & Mohamed, 2018). Sadly, this occurs not only in US media but also in media across the globe, with migrants cast as economic opportunity and asylum seekers, terrorists, and threats to broader state interests (Benson & Wood, 2015; Farris & Mohamed, 2018; Innes, 2010). The consequences of such framing is the normalizing of extreme anti-immigration claims (D'Amato & Lucarelli, 2019) and the dehumanization of migrants (Esses et al., 2013), which, in turn, significantly impact public opinion and policy-making on migration policy issues (Benson & Wood, 2015; Blinder & Allen, 2016; Hallin, 2015; Thorbjørnsrud, 2015).

Despite this, not all actors or all media coverage place migrants in a negative light. Non-profits, global aid groups, and journalists do attempt to give voice to migrant perspectives, often through human interest stories. Thus, whereas government sources tend to dominate immigration news coverage and emphasize the larger problems it may pose to society, pro-immigration associations and unaffiliated individuals showcase the causes of migration and the travails migrants themselves experience (Benson & Wood, 2015). Unfortunately, the battle over public attention regarding migration policies often results in opposing monologues, with such discourse not reflecting societal views but an outcome of journalistic practices and sources' rhetorical strategies. As Ihlen et al. (2015) argues, despite immigration authorities enjoying easy access to leading media, they struggle to find media strategies capable of balancing the messaging constraints imposed by bureaucratic regulations with values of journalistic norms emphasizing dramatic individual stories. NGOs, on the other hand, use this as an opportunity to exploit media conventions and pitch emotional, individual stories to journalists. Still, for both, the challenge is to expand the media interest beyond such stories to foster a systemic debate on immigration policy.

Evaluating, then, the structure of individual and community narratives is an important factor in crafting intelligible migrant policy. As Benson and Wood (2015) argue, within our media landscapes, whose views are cited influences how migration issues are reported and implicate the manner in which news stories about migration are constructed. Hence, debates on migration policy may best be conceptualized as policy narratives setting out beliefs about policy problems and appropriate interventions, which, in turn, draw upon and are comprised of competing values and knowledge claims about the causes, dynamics, and impacts of migration (Boswell et al., 2011). These dynamics then unfold and are contended within media, with dominant, recurring elements resulting in the coalescence of a constellation of symbols and culturally bounded stories that define a political communities' worldview(s) about the issue, both regarding what is possible or imaginable, and what is not.

For these reasons, this chapter explores the underlying structural elements of news reporting on migration over the past 20 years from US, Mexican, and NT media. Whereas the previous chapter uncovered the prominent thematic storylines of such coverage, here we take more of a bird's eye view to unveil to both policy makers and the public the general tendencies and patterns of news coverage reporting on migration. In doing so, our aim is to make such patterns visible to these political communities so that they can both recognize the differences among their reporting tendencies as well as reflect on, and, hopefully, overcome, their own biases in service toward a more cooperative, compassionate, and efficacious discussion and making of policy.

In the remainder of this chapter, we begin by briefly overviewing the chapter's methodology before presenting our findings. We then conclude by discussing the implications of our results as they speak to the differences and similarities regarding the causal claims, elements of exclusion–inclusion, phenomenon of interests, and the constraints and overlays of possible imagined outcomes associated with news reporting on migration.

Method

To trace the structural shifts in news reporting across 20 years of US, Mexican, and NT news reporting, we trained a machine learning algorithm to categorize content along eight variables: region of origin, nation responsible, voices presented, argument type, migrant emotion, perception of migrants, reasons for migration, and discussion of government policies and migrant journey/paths. These eight elements were chosen for their ability to portray the (dis)similar phenomenon of interests within the coverage of migration-related issues. All articles were broken down into five-sentence windows with only those mentioning "migrant," "immigrant," or variants of the two words classified. For a complete discussion of the method, see Chapter 2.

In the findings presented next, we lay out the comparisons of frequencies and trends among US, Mexican, and NT media broken down into four time periods. Time Period 1 includes discussions one year before and after the US Congress' passing of the 2000 Legal Immigration Family Equity Act. Time Period 2 includes the 2005 to 2007 US House and Senate debates on immigration. Time Period 3 spans one year before and after the 2012 DACA and 2013 Gang of Eight debates. Finally, Time Period 4 represents coverage more broadly from 2015 to 2019, representing the lead-up to Donald Trump's presidency and most of his tenure. Comparisons of NT media presentations are limited to Time Periods 2–4, due to constraints on data collection from NT media sources prior to 2000.

Findings

Region of Migrant Origin

Region of migrant origin includes discussions on where migrants are leaving from. Here, we find that Mexican media most frequently discussed the origin of migrants, doing so in 25.7% of coded segments averaged across all four time periods. NT did so with the second highest frequency, at 16.5%, and the US in only 3.6%. Across all countries, references to the origin of migrants increases overtime, rising on average from 2.8% in Period 2 to 3.4% in Period 3, and 4.8% in Period 4.

The increased attention of migrants' area of origin comes from greater discussion of their originating within NT countries and transnational contexts, while references to Mexican migrants sharply decline over time. Thus, whereas 22.2% of coded segments in Mexican media referenced Mexico as the origin of migrants in Period 1, by Period 4 this number dropped to 10.6%. Likewise, US media in Period 1 referenced Mexico as the origin of migration in 3.6% of coded segments, with this number decreasing to 1.4% in Period 4. In contrast, Mexican media increasingly referenced NT as the origin of migrants, doing so at 1.7% in Period 1 compared with 4.3% in Period 4. In US media, only 0.3% of coded segments in Period 1 referred to migrants originating in NT compared to 0.8% in Period 4. In NT media, we see the sharpest rise, with 1.0% of coded segments referencing migrants coming from their region in Period 2, while growing to 9.9% in Period 3, and reaching 16.5% in Period 4.

Furthermore, the data shows an increased recognition of migrants as not necessarily nation-bounded, but originating more broadly in transnational contexts. This shift is most evident in NT media, where references to migrants'

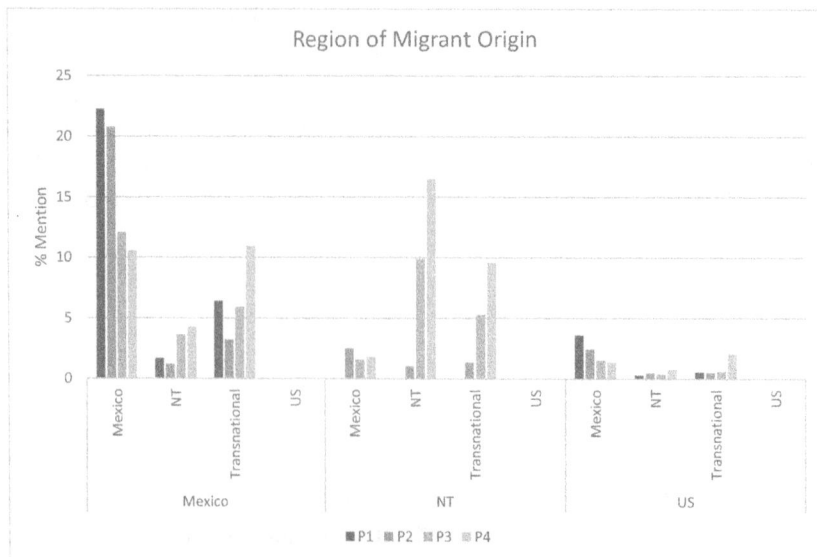

Region of Migrant Origin

transnational origins increase in each period: 1.3% in Period 2, 5.3% in Period 3, and 9.6% in Period 4. US and Mexican media also show large increases in references to migrants' transnational origins, but with this shift occurring primarily in Period 4.

Finally, we see Mexican media most frequently discussing migrants from Mexico—doing so on average and across time periods in 16.4% of coded segments, compared to NT media referencing Mexican migrants at 1.9% and US media doing so at 2.2%. Likewise, NT media discussed migrants originating from the NT on average across time periods in 9.1% of coded segments, compared to Mexico doing so in 2.7% and the US in 0.5%.

Responsibility for Managing Migration

Responsibility for managing migration includes references attributing which government or societal group is charged with addressing causes of migration. As such, across the three regions and time periods, the US was widely viewed as the primary actor needing to take action. US responsibility was referenced on average in 18.0% of coded segments within Mexican media, 26.8% in NT, and 28.1% in the US. In contrast, the NT was rarely seen as the region or country needing to resolve migration issues, with only 0.1% of coded segments in Mexican media placing responsibility on NT countries, 0.05% of US segments doing so, and 0.6% by NT. Mexico falls in the middle, with Mexican media most frequently placing responsibility on themselves—doing so on average in 14.7% of coded segments—followed by NT media placing responsibility on Mexico in 7.1% of their coded segments, and the US in 1.7%.

Trends relating to the shifting burden of responsibility are unclear or remain largely the same. For instance, only in NT media was there a clear increase in placing responsibility within a transnational framework, rising from 1.0% in Period 2 to 13.9% in Period 4. In contrast, Mexican media showed a slight decrease in references to transnational responsibility, with 12.6% of coded segments doing so in Period 1 and 11.3% in Period 2, and dropping to 5.7% in Period 3, before ticking back up to 11.0% in Period 4. Similarly, in US media, references to transnational responsibility in Period 1 occur in 2.0% of coded segments and dip to 1.0% and 0.7% in Periods 2 and 3 respectively, before rising to 1.7% in Period 4.

Nonetheless, US responsibility appears to decline over time in both Mexican and NT media, while increasing slightly in US media. Thus, whereas in Period

1 Mexico placed the burden on the US in 24.4% of coded segments, in Period 4, the number drops to 15.9%. Likewise, in NT media, the number falls from 31.4% in Period 1 to 26.3% in Period 4. In contrast, the US views itself as increasingly responsible, moving from 24.5% in Period 1 to 27.5% in Period 2, and 29.5% in Period 3 to 30.9% in Period 4. Indeed, the US appears to be at odds with Mexican and NT media in overwhelmingly viewing themselves, and only themselves, as responsible for managing migration. Whereas Mexican media references Mexico, NT, or transnational actors in 8.3% of coded segments on average across time periods, with NT media doing so in 4.6% of coded segments, the US references actors other than themselves on average across time in only 1.0% of coded segments.

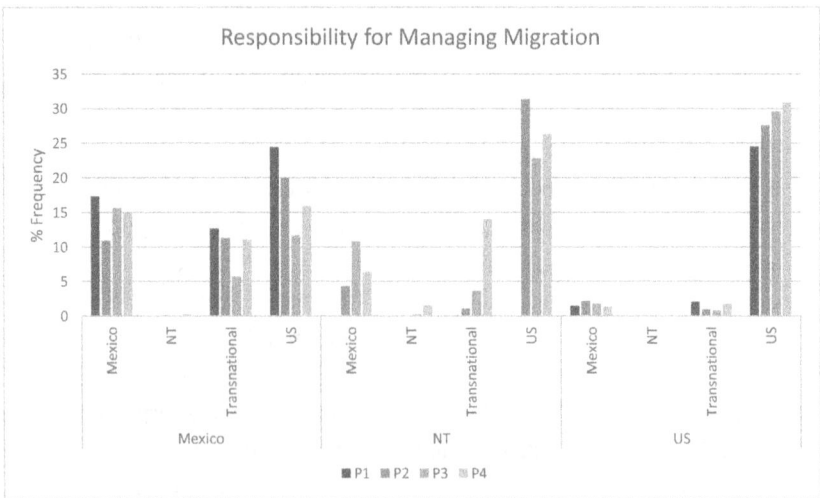

Voices Reported

Voices reported measures what groups are discussed in news articles and thus who or what type of actors makes up the news content and points of views discussed. As such, our data shows that across all three countries/regions, the two predominate voices in coverage on migration were (1) news and (2) politicians. Indeed, the average frequency of coded segments discussing these two groups (from all three countries/regions across time), compared to the other four groups, highlights the first two groups' dominance in coverage, with 15.4% of coded segments mentioning the latter and only 3.0% the former.

More specifically, averaged across time, news sources or journalists are referenced in 24.8% of coded segments in US media, 16.8% in NT media, and 16.0% in Mexican media. Politicians—again averaged across time—are referenced in 10.4% of coded segments in US media, 12.2% in NT media, and 11.9% in Mexican media.

However, whereas articles including news sources remained relatively high across time periods, political voices rose substantially in NT and US media in Period 4. Thus, in NT media, politicians were referenced in 10.2% and 10.1% in Periods 2 and 3, but jump to 16.4% in Period 4. Similarly, in US media, references to politicians increased slightly in Periods 1–3, making up 7.9%, 8.1%, and 9.3% of articles respectively, but jumped to 16.2% in Period 4.

The third most frequent voice referenced on average across time in Mexican and NT media are non-US government agencies, at 9.8% and 7.4%, respectively. In contrast, only 3.5% of coded segments in US articles discussed non-US government agencies, suggesting some level of similarity in Mexican and NT media and dissimilarity in US media, with US media discourse appearing less cognizant, or interested, of actions taken by foreign governments in response to migration. Instead, for US media, migrant voices were the third most frequent voice included in coverage—showing up in 8.3% of coded segments averaged across time, compared to 5.3% in Mexican media and 6.6% in NT media.

Other less frequently discussed voices included aid and religious groups, as well as US government agencies. Averaged across time, aid groups were referenced in 3.3% of coded segments in NT articles, 2.9% in Mexican articles, and 2.5% in US articles; and religious groups were referenced in 1.1%, 1.0%, and 0.7% of coded segments, respectively. US government agencies, despite their active roles in US immigration enforcement, were only referenced in 1.2% of NT articles, 1.1% of Mexican articles, and 1.4% of US articles.

Regarding shifts in the voices present over time, US media decreases its average inclusion of migrant voices with the highest average frequency in Period 1 at 10.4%, which gradually falls in Periods 2–4 (8.7%, 7.8%, and 6.3%, respectively). In contrast, migrant voices remain relatively stable across time in Mexican media (Period 1: 4.9%; Period 2: 4.7%; Period 3: 6.0%; Period 4: 5.5%) and NT media (Period 2: 6.5%; Period 3: 6.8%; Period 4: 6.6%). Instead, US media increases its inclusion of US government agencies, rising from 0.9% in Period 1 to 1.0% in Period 2, 1.2% in Period 3, and 2.5% in Period 4. Other notable shifts include decreases in inclusion of religious groups within NT media, falling from 1.9% in Period 2 to 0.7% and 0.5% in Periods 3 and 4, respectively, as well as increased inclusion of aid groups in Mexican media from 1.3% and 1.9% in Periods 1 and 2 to 4.1% and 4.2% in Periods 3 and 4.

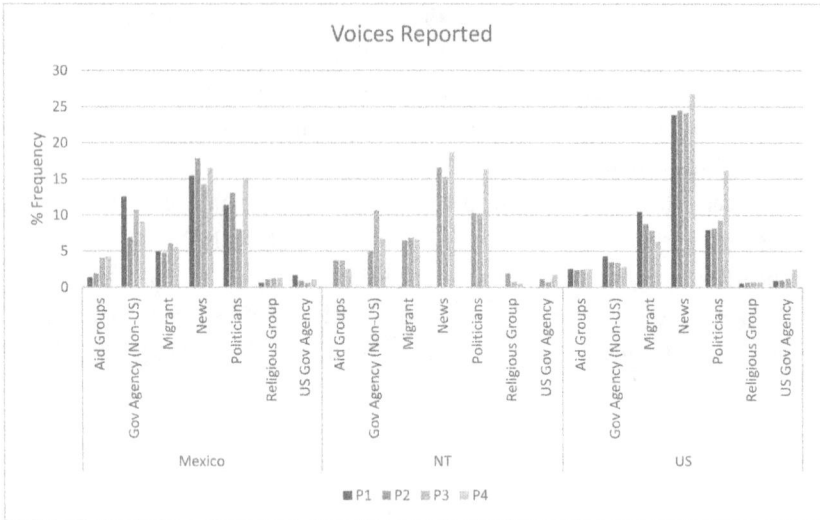

Voices Reported

Argument Type

Argument type reflects reporting's focus on policy, or the logical consequences of cause and effect issues related to migration issues. Emotional characterizations, in contrast, focus on topics like migrant plight, humanitarian issues, and personalized issues. Across all three regions, logic/policy issues were more than twice as likely to be discussed over emotional dimensions of migration. This emphasis on logical policy discussion was most frequent in Mexican media, which—averaged across time periods—shows up in 74.7% of coded segments, followed by NT media in 66.7%, and US media with 63.9%. In both NT and US media, logic/policy argumentation increases over time, while Mexican media also trends higher in this category, but there was a slight decrease in Period 2 (77.2%) to Period 3 (75.5%), before ending higher in Period 4 (77.9%).

Mexican media, however, also shows an increase in emotionally driven articles. Such stories occurred in 13.1% of coded segments in Period 1, 16.4% in Period 2, 19.0% in Period 3, and 20.5% in Period 4. In US and NT media, elements of emotional focus remained relatively stable, with frequencies in US media being 25.0% in Period 1; 25.8% in Period 2; 21.7% in Period 3; and 27.1% in Period 4. Frequencies in NT media were as follows: 22.8% in Period 2; 21.2% in Period 3; and 23.7% in Period 4.

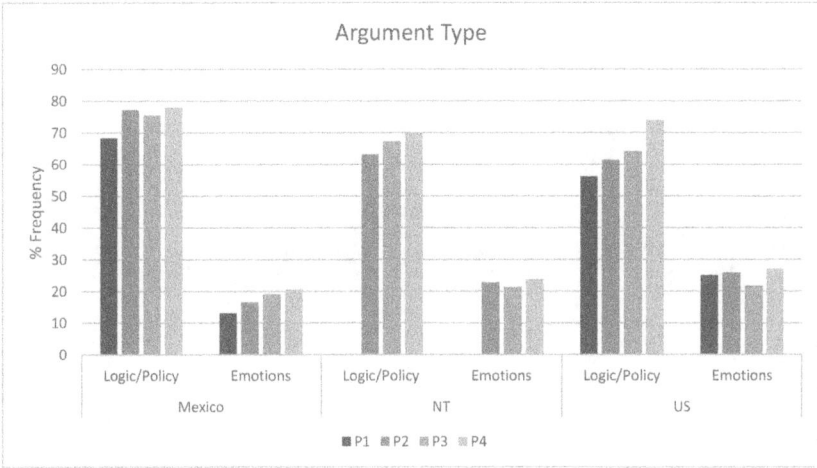

Argument Type

Y-axis: % Frequency (0 to 90)

Groups: Mexico (Logic/Policy, Emotions), NT (Logic/Policy, Emotions), US (Logic/Policy, Emotions)

Legend: ■ P1 ■ P2 ■ P3 ■ P4

Migrant Emotions

When comparing reporting of migrants' affective states, the predominate emotions discussed were feelings of vulnerability/fear/despair. Averaged across time periods, this emotion was reported in 4.2% of coded segments in NT media, 4.1% within Mexican media, and 3.8% within US. Interestingly, US media was the only one to decrease its references to migrant feelings of vulnerability, fear, and despair over time, steadily dropping from 5.0% in Period 1, to 3.9% in Period 2, 3.2% in Period 3, and 3.1% in Period 4. In contrast, we see an increase in NT media references to this emotion from Period 2 (4.1%) to Period 4 (4.8%), while Mexican media remained relatively stable in its reporting of the emotion.

In NT and Mexican media, the second most frequent emotion was disappointment. Averaged across time, this feeling was reported in 1.4% of coded segments within Mexican articles and 2.3% of NT articles. US media referenced humiliation/disregard (0.8%) slightly more often than disappointment (0.7%). Other trends are unclear or remain relatively stable across time periods.

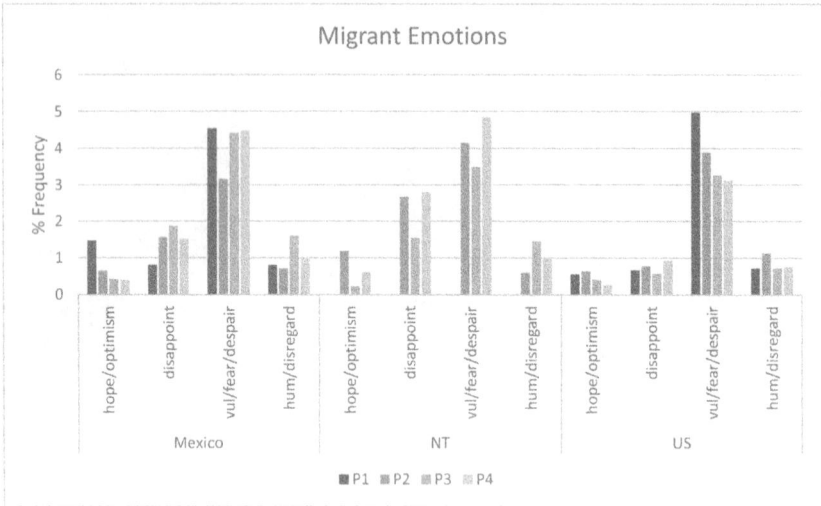

Migrant Emotions

Perceptions of Migrants

Across all three regions, migrants were viewed overwhelmingly in a neutral characterization, that is, neither good nor bad, or having a mix of positive and negative elements. Indeed, averaged across time periods, Mexican and NT media both presented migrants in a neutral manner in 93.4% of coded segments and 89.3% within US segments. Furthermore, such characterizations appear relatively stable, with the lowest frequency in Mexican media being 92.6% and the highest being 93.7%. Likewise, the lowest frequency in NT articles is 91.3% and the highest, 94.5%. US media, on the other hand, shows a slight decrease in neutral characterization, moving from 91.3% in Period 1 to 87.9% in Period 4.

Despite the overwhelming tendencies for migrants to be neutrally characterized, they were more likely to be viewed in a negative, rather than a positive, light. Averaged across time periods, migrants were negatively characterized most often in US media at 8.9%, followed by NT media at 5.3% and Mexican media at 5.1%. Furthermore, whereas negative characterization of migrants remained steady in Mexican media, US media increasingly casts migrants negatively over time, beginning at 7.3% in Period 1 and growing to 10.2% in Period 4. Thus, positive characterizations were few, with only 1.8% of coded segments in US articles, 1.5% in Mexican articles, and 1.3% in NT articles showing clearly positive characterizations.

Perception of Migrants

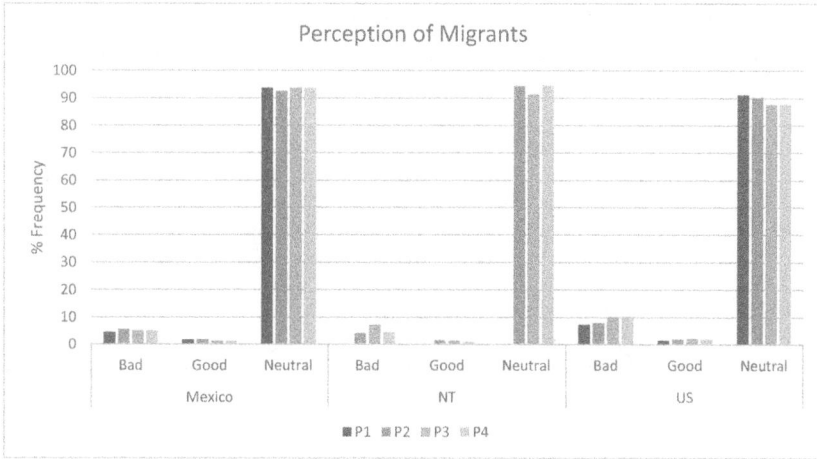

Reasons for Migration

All three countries/regions reported economic causes as the primary reason for migration, with US media doing so in 20.7% of coded segments averaged across time, Mexican media in 17.2% of coded segments, and 15.3% in NT media. However, the data shows sharp falls in economic issues reported in Period 4, both in US and Mexican media. Thus, in Mexican media, economic reasons peaked in Period 2 at 26.3% while falling to 13.6% in Period 4. Likewise, in US media, economic reasons peaked in Periods 2 and 3 (both at 23.9%) and fell to 13.8% in Period 4. In contrast, economic reasons remained relatively stable in NT articles, ranging from 14.7% to 16.0%.

The second most frequent reason for migration was crime/violence, shared by all three countries, albeit with US media doing so substantially less than NT and Mexican media. Averaged across time, 17.2% of coded segments in Mexican articles referenced crime/violence as a reason for migration, compared to 13.8% in NT articles and 9.9% of US articles.

As economic motivators declined over time in Mexican media, discussion of humanitarian concerns and health care all increased in Period 1 to Period 4, from 2.4% to 7.1% and from 2.7% to 4.7%, respectively. In NT media, however, we see steady increases in references to family (5.3% in Period 2 to 9.2% in Period 4), political failure (1.9% in Period 2 to 5.1% in Period 4), and crime/violence (11.4% in Period 2 to 15.9% in Period 4) as the reported motivators. In US media, few substantial shifts are evident outside of decreasing discussion of access to health care (4.9% in Period 1 to 3.3% Period 4), suggesting relative stability in how US media covers migrants' motivation for leaving their countries.

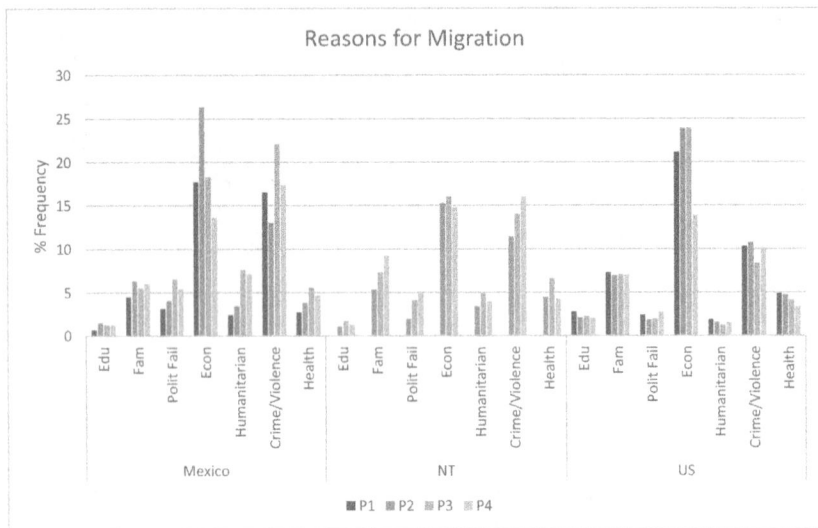

Journey and Policies

Finally, we trained our algorithm to identify articles mentioning specific government policies about migration as well as references to migrants' journeys. Here, we find that despite all three countries/regions frequently reporting on policies to stem migration, both Mexican and NT media report increasing numbers of stories regarding migrant paths. As such, articles referring to specific government policies regarding migration increased over time: in Mexican media, from 38.0% in Period 1 to 50.7% in Period 4; in NT media, from 42.0% in Period 1 to 53.4% in Period 4; and in US media, from 33.2% in Period 1 to 53.9% in Period 4.

Shifts in references to migrant paths are less uniform but can still be seen as increasing from Periods 1 and 2 to Periods 3 and 4 in both Mexican and NT media. In NT media, the number grows from 25.0% (Period 2) to 33.8% (Period 3) to 35.0% (Period 4); in Mexican media, Periods 1 and 2 reference migrant journeys in 30.2% and 29.7% of articles, with references peaking in Period 3 at 40.2%, and dipping slightly in Period 4 to 37.6%. In contrast, US media references to migrants' journeys remained relatively stable across all four periods,

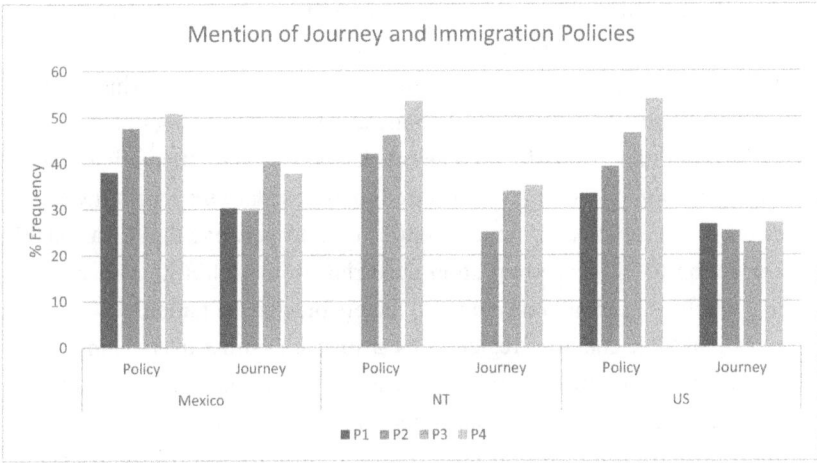

Mention of Journey and Immigration Policies

beginning at 26.7% in Period 1, before dipping in Periods 2 and 3 (25.3% and 22.7%, respectively), and then returning to around 27.0% in Period 4.

Discussion

Taken together, our results demonstrate elements of both change and continuity within NT, Mexican, and US media reporting on migration issues, as well as areas of similarity and dissimilarity among the three countries/regions. We conclude by discussing what these descriptive patterns indicate regarding the three countries/regions' causal claims about migration, elements of exclusion–inclusion, phenomenon of interests, and constraints of possible imagined outcomes.

Casual Claims

First, we can infer some similarities and differences regarding casual claims about migration by turning to which country is viewed as responsible for managing it. In sum, all three countries/regions see the US as the one most capable of creating change, or impacting migration. Indeed, in absolute terms, all three identify the US as the primary nation responsible. However, differences emerge when turning to the changes in frequencies regarding claims of responsibility. Here, Mexican media, in particular, but NT media, as well, place less responsibility on the US overtime, with Mexican media emphasizing its own responsibility in a stable and frequent manner throughout the four Periods of analysis. Furthermore, Mexican and NT media appear to see transnational dynamics as increasingly important causal factors, with NT media, in particular, sharply increasing its references for transnational responsibility. This suggests that, for NT countries, transnational cooperation is an ever important driver of managing migration, while Mexico reports itself as, at least attempting, toward action as well. Finally, as none of the three countries place responsibility on NT countries, it appears that all three countries/regions perceive the NT as unable to take action to influence migration occurring from within its own borders, placing greater causal inference on pull factors outside the nation.

Second, all three countries/regions appear to share similar overarching depictions of the primary causes of migrants leaving their countries. Here, economic reasons are referenced by all media systems most often, but with US and Mexican media sharply decreasing such references in Period 4. This likely reflects the changing patterns in Mexican migration dynamics, in which economics served as a primary driver in the 1990s and 2000s before economic conditions in Mexico improved and economic conditions in the US declined (Villarreal, 2014). Indeed, economic drivers remain a salient factor in NT media throughout, which may suggest that US perceptions of migration remain stuck within earlier frames of reference to US experiences with Mexican migration from previous decades. Likewise, crime/violence is commonly shared as the second most frequent reason for migration. Most notable, however, is the rise in crime/violence in NT media reporting, suggesting continued destabilization occurring in these countries. As crime/violence is discussed frequently in all three media systems, a key means of addressing migration is policies to protect and safeguard migrants' lives.

Finally, all three countries similarly share increasingly prominent discussion of policies in reference to migration. While our data doesn't indicate whether such policies are succeeding or not, we find increased perceptions regarding the importance of policy when addressing migration issues. Nonetheless, to some extent, we can conclude that despite increased discussion of policy, migrants continue to embark on the journey, perhaps in ways specifically designed to circumvent new constraints on migration pathways.

Exclusion–Inclusion

Regarding exclusion–inclusion dynamics relating to migration discussion, first, we see the high degree of logic/policy-oriented discussion, compared to emotional dynamics of coverage, placing migrants more often outside of discussion.

The increase in such argument types further suggests a bureaucratization of migration processes that exclude migrants from policy discussion (Hiemstra & Conlon, 2017; Maher & Segrave, 2018). Furthermore, although Mexican media shows increasing frequencies of emotional elements in their reporting, trends in the NT and US media remain stable. This might suggest that Mexican redresses to migration are shifting toward more inclusive practices and understanding of migrants but that such patterns are not occurring in US or NT media.

Second, clearest indications of migrant exclusion come from their reported emotions. First, on the whole, little coverage includes discussions of migrants' affective state, providing further evidence of the policy-oriented focus on migration discussion to the detriment of more human-oriented concerns of migrants' lives (Greenberg & Hier, 2001; Kim et al., 2011; Suro, 2008). Indeed, when migrants' affective states are covered by the media, it includes depictions of migrants as vulnerable, in fear, or expressing despair. While our data doesn't point to the causes of these feelings, they can be understood as manifestations of their exclusion from society. Further evidence of migrant exclusion comes from their feelings of disappointment; whereas migrants may have left their countries with hope or optimism for a better life, such beliefs appear not to manifest and thus result in their disillusionment or negative feelings of the migration journey, process, or new life.

Third, migrants' dissatisfaction appears somewhat mirrored by US society, which possesses the highest negative perception of migrants. Despite US highs in negative perceptions of migrants, no country perceives migrants in more of a positive than negative light. Instead, they are largely seen in a neutral or mixed manner. While the data regarding migrant perceptions doesn't fully suggest their exclusion from society, they do appear at least not fully included. While drivers of negative perceptions of migration are situational, a likely reason may be the costs incurred on their emigration when leaving their countries of origin and/or the instability—albeit not intended or arising from their individual fault—of their journey through other nations (Verkuyten, 2021). Indeed, as migrants travel, they are often forced underground, require aid, and get caught up in illicit activity as they experience broken immigration systems (UNODC, 2022). Furthermore, the political communities from which migrants leave may also hold migrants in a neutral or negative light through feelings of abandonment as those migrating may be seen as giving up on their native countries or place of birth, even if society recognizes the migrants' reasons for doing so.

Phenomenon of Interests

With regard to phenomenon of interest, our data suggests that, first, there exist similarities in the trends of migrants' country of origin but differences regarding the amount of attention placed on the subject. Regarding the former, all three countries/regions report a decrease in references to migration originating from Mexico but an increase in origins from both NT countries and transnational contexts. This result appears to align with current events, as in Period 4, migrants from NT were the most prevalent origin sources and journeyed through Mexico to the US, while the number of Mexican migrants coming to the US has been on the decline (Cohn et al., 2017). However, despite the similarity in the trends of migrants' shifting country of origin, Mexican and NT media express greater concern as to where migrants originate from, while such discussion is considerably lacking in US media. A possible explanation for this is that individual countries/regions are more interested in covering migrants' countries of origin as they relate to their own populace, as is evident from Mexican media reporting migrants originating from Mexico relatively more frequently than those from the NT and, similarly, from NT media referencing migrants from NT relatively more frequently than those originating from Mexico. Thus, migrant flows out of one's nation is likely to have significant consequences for that nation and can serve as a symptom of broader issues or concerns as driving them to exit—perhaps, engendering broader and more frequent discussion of the causes and implications of these flows when exiting their own countries.

Second, we can infer that the voices reported are evidence of what issues or phenomena are of greatest interest. Here, we find elites dominating the coverage with concerns over politicians' statements and actions as well as journalists' reporting of events taking center stage. As such, these two groups receive the highest media attention across all three countries/regions. Consequently, the narratives circulating within these three media systems appear to be concerned less about migrants themselves and more about the actions by politicians in response to migration issues, which past research suggests shifts focus to broader societal issues rather than migrants' individualized experiences (Greenberg & Hier, 2001; Kim et al., 2011; Suro, 2008). Furthermore, although US media most frequently include migrants' voices in their coverage, this exposure declines over time and thus silences migrants even when their journeys become increasingly dangerous (MSF, 2020). Moreover, the US decline in coverage of migrant voices coincides with all three countries' increasing coverage of politicians, specifically in Period 4, and likely reflects the increased politicization of migration during the Trump administration in the US.

Additional conclusions from our data suggest differences in visibility regarding non-US government agencies' actions in relation to migration, with both Mexican and NT media featuring them relatively prominently but with less discussion of them in US media. This may provide further evidence of US' focus on its own actions and capabilities to the detriment of reporting how other nations' governments are taking steps, whether for good or for bad, toward handling migration issues. Finally, pro-migrant groups, like Aid or Religious organizations are rarely mentioned. Thus, it appears that their actions and statements have less influence or little newsworthiness—compared to coverage of current events or political statements and announcement of policies—and are often drowned out by journalists and politicians. This has implications for such aid and religious groups' ability to rally support for migrants and shape the overarching news agenda, likely in more positive ways.

Imaginative Constraints and Overlays of the Possible

Finally, when reflecting on the constraints and overlaying of possible action regarding migration, our data shows, first, the lack of discussion within US media regarding where migrants are originating from as suggesting a tendency of US media to focus on migration as an action—or the arrival of migrants at the US border as the primary issue of concern, rather than directing attention to the dynamics within the migrants' countries of origin that result in migrants leaving their home countries. Such reporting, then, may constrain support for US policy to address issues within other nations. However, the increased reference to migrants as originating within a transnational context may help drive recognition for policies to address it as such, or at least lay the foundational awareness of doing so in future.

Second, however, when turning to discussions regarding responsibility for managing migration, US media appears to see itself increasingly as the sole agent addressing the issue. Although none of the three countries/regions report NT countries as responsible, perhaps placing them in more of an object than subject frame, Mexican media reports shared responsibility, including frequent references to itself, transnational action, and the US; NT media, on the other hand, shows sharp increases in transnational elements of responsibility, while the US largely ignores both Mexican and transnational obligations for managing migration. This suggests continued constraints on transnational cooperation and continued unilateral steps taken by the US. While the US is indeed the country with the most resources and capabilities to manage migration, viewing it in a one-dimensional frame may lead to less community-oriented solutions in preference for those serving US interests. Likewise, the lack of responsibility placed on NT countries can dangerously abrogate calls for improving or focusing attention on how these governments can or should improve conditions within their own borders to mitigate their citizens' impetus for leaving.

Third, the overwhelming focus on policy, politicians, journalists, and logically driven reports on migration all suggests a tendency toward a bureaucratization of migration, crowding out more human-oriented assessments. This pattern, when taken in context with the narrative themes in the previous chapter, demonstrates more of a concern with deterring migrants rather than caring for them as individuals. Such actions threaten to overpoliticize the issue, leading to less effective policy-making, which ignores the humanitarian dimension of migration as well as failing to address root causes, further exacerbating tensions between migrants and societies, as well as fueling illegal migration (Bermeo, 2019).

REFERENCES

Bermeo, S. (2019, April 3). Central Americans need less violence, more development, and a safe place to stay. *Brookings.* https://www.brookings.edu/blog/future-development/2019/04/03/central-americans-need-less-violence-more-development-and-a-safe-place-to-stay/

Benson, R., & Wood, T. (2015). Who says what or nothing at all? Speakers, frames, and frameless quotes in unauthorized immigration news in the United States, Norway, and France. *American Behavioral Scientist, 59*(7), 802–821. https://doi.org/10.1177/0002764215573257

Blinder, S., & Allen, W. L. (2016). Constructing immigrants: Portrayals of migrant groups in British national newspapers, 2010–2012. *International Migration Review, 50*(1), 3–40. https://doi.org/10.1111/imre.12206

Boswell, C., Geddes, A., & Scholten, P. (2011). The role of narratives in migration policy-making: A research framework. *The British Journal of Politics and International Relations, 13*(1), 1–11. https://doi.org/10.1111/j.1467-856X.2010.00435.x

Castells, M. (2008). The new public sphere: Global civil society, communication networks, and global governance. *The Annals of the American Academy of Political and Social Science, 616*(1), 78–93. https://doi .org/10.1177/0002716207311877

Castells, M. (2009). *The Rise of the Network Society.* Wiley-Blackwell.

D'Amato, S., & Lucarelli, S. (2019). Talking migration: Narratives of migration and justice claims in the European migration system of governance. *The International Spectator, 54*(3), 1–17. https://doi.org/10.1080/03932729.2019. 1643181

Cohn, D., Passel, J. S., & Gonzalez-Barrera, A. (2017, December 7). *Rise in U.S. immigrants from El Salvador, Guatemala and Honduras outpaces growth from elsewhere.* Pew Research Center. https://www.pewresearch.org/hispanic/2017/12/07/rise-in-u-s-immigrants-from-el-salvador-guatemala-and-honduras-outpaces-growth-from-elsewhere/

Esses, V. M., Medianu, S., & Lawson, A. S. (2013). Uncertainty, threat, and the role of the media in promoting the dehumanization of immigrants and refugees. *Journal of Social Issues, 69*(3), 518–536. https://doi.org/10.1111 /josi.12027

Farris, E. M., & Silber Mohamed, H. (2018). Picturing immigration: how the media criminalizes immigrants. *Politics, Groups, and Identities, 6*(4), 814–824. https://doi.org/10.1080/21565503.2018.1484375

Gilboa, E., Jumbert, M. G., Miklian, J., & Robinson, P. (2016). Moving media and conflict studies beyond the CNN effect. *Review of International Studies, 42*(4), 654–672. https://doi.org/10.1017/S026021051600005X

Greenberg, J., & Hier, S. (2001). Crisis, mobilization and collective problematization: "Illegal" Chinese migrants and the Canadian news media. *Journalism Studies, 2*, 563–583. https://doi.org/10.1080/14616700120086413

Hallin, D. C. (2015). The dynamics of immigration coverage in comparative perspective. *American Behavioral Scientist, 59*(7), 876–885. https://doi .org/10.1177/0002764215573259

Harris, C. T., & Gruenewald, J. (2020). News media trends in the framing of immigration and crime, 1990–2013. *Social Problems, 67*(3), 452–470. https:// doi.org/10.1093/socpro/spz024

Hiemstra, N., & Conlon, D. (2017). Beyond privatization: Bureaucratization and the spatialities of immigration detention expansion. *Territory, Politics, Governance, 5*(3), 252–268. https://doi.org/10.1080/21622671.2017.1284693

Ihlen, Ø., Figenschou, T. U., & Larsen, A. G. (2015). Behind the framing scenes: Challenges and opportunities for NGOs and authorities framing irregular immigration. *American Behavioral Scientist, 59*(7), 822–838. https://doi .org/10.1177/0002764215573254

Innes, A. J. (2010). When the threatened become the threat: The construction of asylum seekers in British media narratives. *International Relations, 24*(4), 456–477. https://doi.org/10.1177/0047117810385882

Kim, S.-h., Carvalho, J. P., Davis, A. G., & Mullins, A. M. (2011). The view of the border: News framing of the definition, causes, and solutions to illegal immigration. *Mass Communication and Society, 14*, 292–314. https://doi .org/10.1080/15205431003743679

Maher, J., & Segrave, M. (2018). Family violence risk, migration status and 'vulnerability': hearing the voices of immigrant women. *Journal of gender-based violence, 2*(3), 503–518. https://doi.org/10.1332/23986801 8X15375304047178

MSF. (2020, February 11). *Escaping violence into danger – no way out for Central American migrants.* https://www.msf.org/escaping-violence -danger-no-way-out-central-american-migrants-mexico

Thorbjørnsrud, K. (2015). Framing irregular immigration in western media. *American Behavioral Scientist, 59*(7), 771–782. https://doi .org/10.1177/0002764215573255

Suro, R. (2008). *The triumph of no: How the media influence the immigration debate.* Brookings Institution. https://www.brookings.edu/wp-content/up-loads/2012/04/0925_immigration_dionne.pdf

United Nations Office on Drugs and Crime. (2022). *Smuggling of migrants: The harsh search for a better life.* https://www.unodc.org/toc/en/crimes/mi-grant-smuggling.html

Verkuyten, M. (2021). Public attitudes towards migrants: Understanding cross-national and individual differences. *World Psychiatry, 20*(1), 132. https:// doi.org/10.1002/wps.20819

Villarreal, A. (2014). Explaining the decline in Mexico-US migration: The effect of the Great Recession. *Demography, 51*(6), 2203–2228. https://doi .org/10.1007/s13524-014-0351-4

## CHAPTER 6

Policy Briefs

Illegal and irregular migration are recognized as problems by most governments and nongovernmental organizations (including the UN). They pose
considerable risks for migrants themselves and present serious issues for destination countries as public safety can be threatened and the rule of law undermined (Dumont et al., 2020; Meissner, 2019). No single policy is ever enough
to address irregular migration since there are a broad range of economic and
social factors in countries of both origin and destination that contribute to this
phenomenon (Dumont et al., 2020). Most governments have developed policies that are targeted at minimizing illegal and irregular migration, some more
effectively than others. This chapter builds on migration policy briefs available
through a number of NGOs, nonprofit organizations, think tanks and educational centers studying migration issues worldwide.

The policy briefs review takes an inductive and interpretive approach. Using
qualitative content analysis, we have systematically analyzed policy briefs, reports, and policy essays published on the subject of migration within the last 5
years (publication dates 2015–2020). A total of fifty-seven policy briefs from
20 organizations are included within this review (See Table 6.1)

Table 6.1: Organizations included in the Policy Documents Review

WOLA	Advocacy for Human Rights in the Americas	www.wola.org
	Bipartisan Policy Center	www.bipartisanpolicy.org
CGD	Center for Global Develop-ment	www.cgdev.org
CSIS	Center for Strategic and Interna-tional Studies	www.csis.org

CFR	Council on Foreign Relations	www.cfr.org
	Creative Associates International	www.creativeassociatesinternational.com
GFMD	Global Forum on Migration and Development	www.gfmd.org
KNO-MAD	Global Knowledge Partnership on Migration and Development	www.knomad.org
ICMPD	International Centre for Migration Policy Development	www.icmpd.org
IOM	International Organization for Migration	www.iom.int
MEDAM	Justice in Mexico	www.justiceinmexico.org
	Mercator Dialogue on Asylum and Migration	www.medam-migration.eu
MPC	Migration Policy Center	www.migrationpolicy-centre.eu
MPI	Migration Policy Institute	www.migrationpolicy.org
	OECD Migration Policy Debates	www.oecd.org/migration
FMUMP	The Forced Migration Upward Mobility Project	www.fmump.org
TCM	Transatlantic Council on Migration	www.migrationpolicy.org
UNHCR	United Nations High Commissioner for Refugees	www.unhcr.org
WZB	World Bank Group	www.worldbank.org
	WZB Berlin Social Science Center	www.wzb.eu

Themes Within Sense-Making Claims

Researchers often engage in categorization and classification of migration-related policies. These attempts have resulted in various typologies that relied on a so-called "national model approach," and these typologies present the ideal types of states (Koopmans, 2013, p. 696). Some of the examples include "idioms of nationhood" (Brubaker, 1992), "models of citizenship" (Safran, 1997), and "citizenship regimes" (Koopmans et al., 2005). These models are often criticized for being too static, simplistic, and normative (Bertossi & Duyvendak, 2012; Finotelli & Michalowski, 2012; Helbling & Vink, 2013) because they rely heavily on simplified distinctions based on "ethnic" versus "civic" citizenship policies (Schmid & Helbling, 2016).

An alternative approach to assessing migration policies is to deviate from classifications and focus instead on developing numerous composite indices measuring migration policies comparatively in a quantitative way (Schmid & Helbling, 2016). An example of such approaches is the Immigration Policies in Comparison (IMPIC) index, which is based on the framework developed by Munck and Verkuilen (2002). The index is derived from a comprehensive theoretical formulation; is empirically validated; and also offers rigorous conceptualization, measurement, and aggregation of data (Schmid & Helbling, 2016). Here, the sense-making claims are linked to the reasons why countries accept migrants, and four distinct "policy fields" emerge: (1) labor migration policies reflecting economic reasons, (2) family reunification policies corresponding to social reasons, (3) refugee and asylum seeker policies pertaining to humanitarian reasons, and, finally, (4) co-ethnics policies reflecting cultural and historical reasons (Schmid & Helbling, 2016).

These policy fields are further differentiated between various sub-groups. For example, labor migration policies are sub-divided into low-skilled, high-skilled, self-employed, and unspecified migrants; family reunification policies are differentiated between sponsors that are citizens versus sponsors that are third-country nationals; asylum policies are sub-divided into policies targeted at recognized refugees, asylum seekers, and people with humanitarian protection; finally, migrant policies in the field of co-ethnics recognize up to four different entry tracks (Schmid & Helbling, 2016). Researchers argue that a clear-cut separation between the policy fields of migration, integration, and citizenship is often difficult (Schmid & Helbling, 2016), yet this classification is valuable in our understanding of the larger picture of migration trends.

Labor Migration Sense-Making Themes

Labor migration policies are often divided into two broad groups: policies that address low-skilled labor migrants and policies that address more skilled migrants. Many of the policies and partnerships between countries focus on the first type, while the second type (focusing on skilled migrants) has only recently been emphasized (largely due to the 2015–2016 refugees and migration crisis in the European Union). We will first review the first type of policies, which address low-skilled labor migrants.

Low-Skilled Labor Migration Policies

Low-skilled labor migrants (also sometimes called "low-waged") often fall through the cracks in policies and frameworks created to protect their ability to immigrate and work in other countries (Newland & Riester, 2018). The reality of the situation in North America and Europe is that these destination countries will continue to have more affluent, educated, and aging populations, which will increase the need for low-skilled workers to fill roles that are deemed undesirable (Newland & Riester, 2018). Steps should be taken to enact the proactive low-skilled labor migration policies because currently, most low-skilled migrants do not move through legal channels (Newland & Riester, 2018). Endorsing the migration-management framework for low-skilled migrants benefits destination countries in three ways. First, improving legal channels could divert large, chaotic mass migrations to more regulated points of entry. Second, more regulation could help curb the death and injury that migrants face when attempting to reach their destination. Finally, an influx of legal workers helps promote growth in the nations they migrate to (Newland & Riester, 2018).

Several suggestions are offered by policy analysts regarding low-skilled labor migration policies. It is important to closely regulate the recruitment and treatment of low-skilled workers, because they are subject to abuse by employers seeking to take advantage of their situation (Newland & Riester, 2018). Ensuring that policies, frameworks, and treaties are clear and flexible is of critical importance. Ambiguity of status, wages, and rights for low-skilled workers puts a strain on livelihoods of migrants and their employers (Newland & Riester, 2018). An emphasis should be placed on a thorough evaluation of migration programs since it will allow countries to adapt their approaches to legal migration channels. This will also ensure that the programs remain as efficient as possible (Newland & Riester, 2018).

Skilled Labor Migration Policies

The second type of migration policies in our review focuses on skilled labor migrants from origin countries to destination countries. Some destination countries (such as Canada, Australia, the United Kingdom, and Singapore) are among major immigrant-receiving countries that have modernized their policies to reposition their systems to identify the workers their economies need to compete in this globalized world, all while benefiting from skilled labor migration. In contrast, other countries (such as the US), have a more "rigid, outdated system for tapping valuable human capital" (Meissner, 2019, p. 2).

Policy analysts argue that origin countries are often reluctant to facilitate skilled migration because of investments in the human capital of their citizens and fears of depleting these stocks (Hooper, 2019). However, origin countries often do benefit from skilled emigration because of remittances and opportunities to develop and transfer new knowledge and skills as well as opportunities to establish new networks for trade and investment (Hooper, 2019). Some skilled migration partnerships have enjoyed great successes (such as the Germany's Triple Win project, which recruits nurses from the Philippines, Serbia, and Bosnia-Herzegovina), while other pilot programs failed. We will further review the factors that contribute to the success of skilled labor migration policies and the areas of improvements.

The Triple Win program is a partnership between Germany's Federal Employment Agency, the Deutsche Gesellschaft für Internationale Zusammenarbeit (GIZ) and governments of Bosnia and Herzegovina, the Philippines, and Serbia. At the heart of the program are well-qualified nurses from origin counties that are unable to find employment in their home countries but whose skills are highly valued and needed in Germany (Pressestelle, 2017). Thus, the program helps to meet the demand for skilled care workers in Germany, eases the pressure on labor markets in the partner countries, and provides benefits to participants through new career opportunities in Germany (Pressestelle, 2017). The success of the program is ensured through language and preparation courses in origin countries "to ensure that those who come to Germany feel at ease in their new linguistic, cultural and working environment" (Pressestelle, 2017).

The UN Global Compact for Safe, Orderly, and Regular Migration proposed a "*global skills partnership*" approach that entails early investments in migration cycle and a focus on training prospective migrants rather than recruiting professionals who are already qualified in their fields (Hooper, 2019; Hooper & Newland, 2018; Clemens, 2015, 2017). The reasoning is as follows: the cost of training one person in a destination country is the same as the cost of training several people to the same standard in an origin country. A 2014 study showed that a three-year professional nursing program in schools in Casablanca, Morocco, and Sousse, Tunisia, would cost 1/7 of a similar program in Germany or

England (Clemens, 2015). After completing training programs, the trainees in origin countries will have a choice of either moving and working in a destination country ("the away track") or staying and choosing to work in their home countries ("the home track") (Hooper, 2019).

The Australia-Pacific Technical College (APTC) is an example of such partnership between Australia and Pacific Island countries. While APTC's training is highly rated by both employers and participants, some questions emerge from this model: how to align training standards among countries; how to deliver training that is beneficial for both destination and origin country employers; and how to distribute the costs of training so they are shared by governments, employers, prospective migrants, and trainees who choose to stay in their home countries (Hooper, 2019).

Another example of the global skill partnership is a program between Belgium and Morocco, where there are investments in training information and communication technology (ICT) workers. Within this program, Belgium has agreed to finance ICT workers in Morocco: some will stay within the Moroccan labor market, while others will migrate to work contracts for Belgian companies (Clemens et al., 2019). The positive impact that global skill partnerships make are in managing future migration pressure, directly involving employers, promoting public–private partnerships, creating skills before migration, promoting development by bundling training for migrants with training for non-migrants in the country of origin, and providing flexibility (adapting to the specific country needs in both destination and origin countries) (Clemens et al., 2019).

There are certain recommendations that policy analysts offer in order to ensure the success of these global skill partnership programs. Some recommendations relate to benefits for origin countries for development purposes. Hooper (2019) suggests careful consideration in providing investments in countries of origin before people move; facilitating skills transfers while people are overseas; and assisting returning migrants in, among other things, putting their skills to good use. Other recommendations include sharing costs with employers, supporting migrants in destinations countries, and sustaining demand for migrant workers in the target sector(s) (Hooper, 2019).

One of the most important recommendations is bringing together a wide array of actors (government and nongovernment) in terms of destination–origin cooperation and working across various policy areas (not just migration) (Hooper & Newland, 2018). A successful example of the cooperation is Porsche's Training and Recruitment Centre in Manila, which trains young Filipinos to work as service or bodywork technicians for Porsche, Volkswagen, or Audi in the

Middle East (Hooper & Newland, 2018). Another center is located in South Africa in Cape Town. According to this program, socially underprivileged young adults pursue two years of vocational education as automotive mechatronics with specialization in high-voltage and digitalization and are then offered employment (Wheels24, 2019). This cooperation is a partnership between Don Bosco Mondo, the local Salesian Institute Youth Projects (SIYP), and the local Porsche importer LSM Distributors (Pty.) Ltd (Wheels24, 2019).

Themes within Exclusion–Inclusion Claims

Exclusion–inclusion claims are centered primarily on the migration policies that address forcibly displaced people (including internally displaced people, refugees, and asylum seekers), who number more than 70 million people worldwide (UNHCR, 2020). Multiple actors and multiple frameworks govern displacement globally and at a regional level, yet the solutions to displacements are often lacking and are not tailored to the needs of the individual (Noack et al., 2020). Not unexpectedly, migration policies addressing the forcibly displaced people vary greatly between developing and developed countries, and that is where the exclusion/inclusion claims play a role. While refugees in North America and Europe are reserved basic human rights, those in lower-income countries struggle to survive. This gap is attributed to three main factors. First, there is an unequal global distribution of responsibility. Next, governments are not willing to extend full rights and benefits to these refugees. Finally, even when destination countries would be willing to offer state protections, they lack the capacity to do so (Fratzke & Le Coz, 2019).

Our review brings us to the analysis of exclusion–inclusion claims in developing countries and later to the investigation of exclusion–inclusion claims in developed countries.

Exclusion–Inclusion Claims in Developing Countries

It is estimated that most of the world's refugees (more than 85%) reside in low- and middle-income countries (UNHCR, 2018). Many of these countries have asylum laws and processes, but they lack the resources to provide refugees with access to already-strained national services (Newland, 2019). Policy analysts argue that these countries require investments in their capacity for service delivery and good governance, similarly to the kinds of investments that development organizations often include in their normal programming (Fratzke & Le Coz, 2019).

Steps to change the current situation require not only extensive planning but also financial and technical support from developmental actors (such as the UN, national development agencies, and development banks) (Fratzke & Le Coz, 2019). These supporters need to work together to assess the current refugee situations and create accurate shared goals. Once needs are assessed, these development actors can focus on generation buy-in with agencies, companies, and ministries that can aid in refugee-related concerns. Investing in the host nations as well as the refugees will help develop their communities (Fratzke & Le Coz, 2019). Development actors recognize that providing immediate aid to refugees is not a sustainable plan and that it can lead to tension with countries that perceive that refugees are being prioritized over their own citizens. A long-term plan too needs to be created by actors specializing in cross-government restructuring (Fratzke & Le Coz, 2019).

As policy makers around the world are looking for more sustainable solutions to refugee crises, one promising approach is to expand economic opportunities for refugees in developing countries (Huang & Graham, 2018). Recently, some innovative ways have been proposed to include governments, donors, and private sector actors to include refugees in labor markets, thus enabling them to become more self-reliant, reducing the cost of hosting refugees and creating economic benefits for hosts (Huang et al., 2018; Huang & Graham, 2018). Some lessons have been learned from these approaches, and recommendations have been provided. First, it is important to define shared outcomes and targets at global and national levels. These collective outcomes and shared targets will ensure that approaches are complementary and have impact (Huang et al., 2018). Second, it is critical to engage a wide range of stakeholders through improved partnership and coordination models. Avoiding duplication of effort, encouraging broader support for projects, promoting learning between stakeholders with different expertise and perspectives would be achieved through this coordination (Huang et al., 2018). Third, conducting joint analysis and planning to align approaches would further streamline the process (Huang et al., 2018). Finally, policy analysts recommend putting in place clear accountability mechanisms, as this will increase transparency on financial flows and their impact (Huang et al., 2018).

Exclusion–Inclusion Claims in Developed Countries

What are some of the exclusion–inclusion claims that policy analysts make within developed countries? Often, they discuss forcibly displayed people and the best practices for inclusion within the system as well as the criteria for exclusion (how to determine the validity of refugee claims). For example, the Migration Policy Institute (MPI) examined the US asylum system and offered recommendations, such as an affirmative system policy "based on principles of timeliness and fairness in providing protection, which will, in turn, discourage unfounded claims and deter opportunistic flows" (Meissner et al., 2018, p. 23). Policy analysts argue that the affirmative system is the most responsive to changes because significant adjustments can be achieved through administrative measures already available to decision makers (Meissner et al., 2018, p. 23). The first recommendation is to restore timeliness—the most effective way to deter misuse while advancing fair treatment of those applying for protection (Bipartisan Policy Center, 2019; Meissner et al., 2018). This could be achieved through building out the "last-in, first-out" processing model for new cases, referring positive credible-fear cases to the asylum division rather than the immigration courts, streamlining credible-fear screening, and referring likely cancellation-of-removal cases to an alternate decision process (Bipartisan Policy Center, 2019; Meissner et al., 2018). The second recommendation is to mobilize regional cooperation to address regional challenges, which can be achieved through deepening engagement and leadership that reduces forced migration from, and among, neighboring countries (Meissner et al., 2018). Such cooperation and collaborations should "promote migration-management regimes that include reception, alternatives to detention, effective asylum adjudication systems within the region; potential processing and resettlement … and durable citizen-security and economic-development solutions" (Meissner et al., 2018, p. 29).

Policy analysts also discuss exclusion–inclusion of forcibly displaced people by addressing the causes of forced displacements, such as corruption, human rights abuses, and other contributing factors (Hinojosa & Meyer, 2019). We identified several manageable steps that address these problems: (a) pressing for strengthening the rule of law, judicial systems, and the protection of children, women, and indigenous populations; (b) supporting reformers and anti-corruption figures, within and outside government, and international anti-corruption mechanisms; (c) standing up for human, environmental, indigenous, and other rights defenders who are pressing their countries to better protect people; and (d) insisting that governments address abuses by security forces and continue efforts to strengthen civilian police forces (Hinojosa & Meyer, 2019).

Germany employed several policy levers to try to manage migration and inclusion/integration challenges associated with asylum seekers and refugees. The cluster asylum processing system has been developed to speed up processing times. It promotes efficiency within the system and enables asylum seekers from countries with high protection rates to access integration services while they wait for their claims to be adjudicated (Brücker et al., 2019). The distribution policy was designed to bind asylum seekers to an obligation to stay in an assigned area for three years and therefore reduce segregation and concentration in certain areas (Brücker et al., 2019). Additionally, a set of integration policies have focused on tailoring integration support to the needs of different groups and increasing service providers' ability to deliver programs at scale. The integration policies focused on access to language training programs, vocational language training, assessments of professional competences and instruction on topics such as the legal system, culture, and values (Brücker et al., 2019). These asylum seekers and refugees policies "marked improvements … in refugees' language skills, personal networks, participation in education and training, and rates of employment" (Brücker et al., 2019, p. 26). Finally, Germany has proven to be successful in directing asylum and refugee migration into labor migration. The German Western Balkan Labor Migration program is an example of such a program. In 2015, Germany received many applications for asylum from people arriving from the Western Balkan area; most of these asylum seekers did not meet the conditions for protection (Dumont et al., 2020). After introducing the program, most of the applicants withdrew their applications, left Germany and re-entered under the new labor migration pathway. The program was the centerpiece of a set of successful interventions to shift flows from the Western Balkans away from the asylum channel, and it showed that a well-designed policy can provide an alternative to use of the asylum system (Dumont et al., 2020).

Other attempts to include/integrate refugees into labor markets resulted in the Intra-Corporate Transferees (ICTs) program within the EU (Hudson, 2020). This distinct category of workers provide services and skills that cannot be found locally, come for a limited amount of time on relatively high salaries, and positively contribute to the destination country from the economic perspective (Hudson, 2020). Experts believe that ICTs will help the EU reach its development goals in areas such as technology, artificial intelligence, and medical advancements (Hudson, 2020).

The two-generation framework is another approach to refugee inclusion/ integration. It was developed by the MPI in 2017 and suggests the need to provide for the children of refugees, strengthening the entire family and not just the individuals alone (Greenberg et al., 2018). Many individual states within the US are already implementing programs aligned with the two-generation approach. For example, Michigan and California have multiple programs that focus on providing refugee kids with child care and schooling, including English lessons. Washington and Colorado have taken steps to provide refugee families with mental and physical health examinations. Funding for these programs typically comes from local governments and business foundations, but there is still a reliance on government support (Greenberg et al., 2018). A series of recommendations for federal and state governments have been developed by the MPI. First, the Bureau of Population, Refugees, and Migration within the US Department of State should, in consultation with voluntary agencies, review and update the requirements and performance outcome measures for the Reception and Placement Program to establish a two-generation/whole-family approach to services delivered (Greenberg et al., 2018). Second, state-wide refugee resettlement programs should identify existing two-generation initiatives currently ongoing within each state's department responsible for human services and ensure that the refugee resettlement network becomes an active partner in such initiatives (Greenberg et al., 2018). Finally, the resettlement agencies should identify existing best practices among offices and programs that reflect principles of two-generation strategies, and ensure that they are shared across the organization and elevated to the attention of state refugee resettlement programs, both in the state in which they operate and in other states (Greenberg et al., 2018).

It is evident from migration research that some refugees become successfully included/integrated in a society, while others struggle to reach living-wage situations. In one policy brief, Dr. Nibbs described this phenomenon. Her bottom-up, refugee-centric study offered several strategies for successful inclusion/integration: tuition-supported living-wage skill trainings, industry-specific ESL[1]-to-vocation classes, career trajectory guidance, strategic initial job placement, and on-the-job training (Nibbs, 2016). These strategies will facilitate upward mobility, increase refugee capacities, speed up economic integration, improve organizational response, eliminate state aid dependency,

---

[1.] English as a Second Language.

fill the long-term needs of today's workforce, and create a more welcoming and empowering environment for newcomers (Nibbs, 2016).

Phenomenon of Interest

This project's efforts identified three phenomena of interest in policy reviews. They are discussed further in this chapter: the phenomenon of circular migration, the phenomenon of return and reintegration, and the phenomenon of refugee sponsorship.

Circular Migration Phenomenon

Circular migration is a relatively new paradigm that is not grounded in more traditional understandings of binary concepts of "permanent" and "temporary" migration (O'Neil, 2003). It is defined as "repeated migration experiences between an origin and destination involving more than one migration and return" (Hugo, 2013). It understands migration as a circular process (migrants return to their origin country, once or many times over a period of time) and as a transitional state (migrants move to migrant communities in the destination country and maintain strong social, business, and political ties to the sending country) (O'Neil, 2003). Circular migration, when properly administered, has the potential to be a win-win situation for both origin and destination countries. For destination countries, circular migration can give flexibility to overcome skill shortages while adapting to long-term market shifts; likewise, origin countries can benefit by giving migrants the opportunity to gain experience and earn higher wages while maintaining valued connections with their homes (Hugo, 2013). One example of circular migration formally established by governments worldwide are seasonal worker programs.

Seasonal worker programs are designed to provide opportunities for low-skilled workers to temporarily migrate from one country to another in order to meet seasonal labor needs in sectors such as agriculture, hospitality or tourism. The US Temporary Foreign Worker Program has been operating since World War I, but it struggled to balance the shifting needs of various sectors and address the concerns of the domestic labor force (Felter, 2019). Additionally, the situation has been complicated by high levels of undocumented immigration and deficiencies in the US government's tracking of visas (Felter, 2019).

Designing and operating seasonal worker programs requires legal frameworks, cooperation between governments, and coordination with a variety of actors such as employers and trade unions. We turn to Europe to learn about their seasonal worker programs as they are seen as one of the solutions to migration issues in Europe, with well-established programs in Germany and the UK. In 2014, the European Union established the Seasonal Workers Directive, which provides common standards for seasonal work and working conditions. It also establishes rules that govern admission and residence of third-country nationals (Hooper & Le Coz, 2020). This directive has three goals: (1) to help meet demand for seasonal labor while curbing illegal employment; (2) to protect the rights of workers; and (3) to provide development benefits for participating countries of origin (Commission of the European Communities, 2005). The established common rules pertained to admission, residence, and rights of non-EU seasonal workers. Some restrictions are posed to migrants, such as the duration of stay in the European Union (five to nine months per year) and limitations for family reunification. Seasonal worker rights are a large part of the directive, which allows migrants to switch employers. Individual countries retain the discretion to decide who and how many migrants to admit, the exact length of their admission (within the five-to-nine–month range), as well as whether and how to facilitate repeat hires (Commission of the European Communities, 2005).

Various European NGOs (such as the MPI and the Expert Council of German Foundations on Integration and Migration) have studied the issue and identified four challenges that are most often associated with seasonal worker programs. By reviewing these challenges, we can emphasize the factors that contribute to successes of seasonal worker programs. First, hiring the right foreign workers at the right time is critical (Hooper & Le Coz, 2020). Swift recruitment procedures are especially important in the agricultural sector because it is difficult to predict size and timing of harvests. Delays in the recruitment or visa approval process can significantly impact the success of seasonal worker programs, as was the case with the US in 2015, when hardware failure left legal farmworkers stranded in Mexico, threatening the harvest of fruit and vegetable farms in the US (Jordan, 2015). Streamlining the process for employers and workers who abide by the rules is the top priority for the success of seasonal worker programs (Hooper & Le Coz, 2020).

The second factor that is a challenge to seasonal worker programs is ensuring that workers play by the rules (Hooper & Le Coz, 2020). The biggest concern from the perspective of destination countries is to ensure that workers return to their countries of origin at the end of their contract. Several solutions have been proposed (and tested) to address this challenge. For example, the Seasonal Workers Directive gives an option to individual countries to require employers to cover their seasonal workers' travel expenses. This practice can help workers avoid incurring debt that can cause them to overstay their visas until they can pay it off (Hooper & Le Coz, 2020). Another example is in New Zealand, where employers are held accountable to cover the cost of removing any of their workers who overstay (Gibson & McKenzie, 2014). Another example is the bilateral labor agreements between France and two African countries (Morocco and Tunisia), where the African countries demonstrated that they are willing to take back their nationals if issued return orders (Hooper & Le Coz, 2020; Natter, 2015).

The third challenge is safeguarding the rights of seasonal workers (Hooper & Le Coz, 2020). Exploitation of workers is of particular concern, in light of multiple documented reports of abuse, underpayment, and extreme work demands and poor living conditions (Corrado, 2017). Researchers provide some promising strategies for reducing exploitation, such as predeparture orientations (organized by either government, trade unions, or employers themselves) with an emphasis on providing workers with detailed information (such as the terms of their employment, the working conditions they should expect, and their rights and options to seek legal remedies in instances of abuse) and access to certain services for foreign workers (such as legal assistance) (Hooper & Le Coz, 2020).

The last challenge, which is also an opportunity, is capitalizing on the close ties between migration and development: maximizing the benefits for seasonal workers and sending countries (Hooper & Le Coz, 2020). Seasonal worker programs are viewed as a win-win solution because they benefit destination countries by meeting their labor needs and origin countries by providing migrants with opportunities to earn higher wages, develop new skills, and gain professional experience (Doyle & Sharma, 2017; Hedberg et al., 2019). Some recommendations have emerged to maximize the potential development impacts of seasonal worker programs. Practitioners recommend enhancing opportunities for countries with lower rates of participation, lowering barriers to participation for more remote areas, focusing recruitment efforts on unemployed labor, and providing financial advice and resources for savings options for seasonal workers on their return (Doyle & Sharma, 2017). Most importantly, researchers stress that the success of these programs hinges on careful policy design that integrates both labor market and development aims (Hugo, 2013; UN General Assembly, 2006).

Refugee Sponsorship Phenomenon

According to policy briefs, refugee sponsorship programs take a variety of forms, while the common element is a transfer of some degree of responsibility (such as identifying and preparing refugees to travel, helping them settle and/or integrating them into a new society) from the government to nongovernment groups (such as private citizens or nonprofit organizations) (Fratzke et al., 2019). These programs differ from country to country, but there are certain commonalities among the most successful sponsorship programs that they possess: (a) interest and support, (b) knowledge, (c) infrastructure, and (d) resources (Fratzke et al., 2019).

The need for interest and support of the refugee sponsorship initiatives is critical toward maintaining effective programs that are consistent in delivering the proper assistance. However, policy analysts maintain that conclusively handing over responsibility to private institutions creates concerns related to delivering services of consistent quality. (Fratzke et al., 2019). Private engagements may be especially advantageous in inciting changes and creating new programs. For instance, the head of the Irish Refugee Protection Programme, in collaboration with the minister of justice and equality, drove the creation of the Community Sponsorship Ireland pilot in 2019. Both parties were highly committed to implementing sponsorship in Ireland (Fratzke et al., 2019).

The second key ingredient for a successful refugee sponsorship program is knowledge. A sponsor should have the necessary knowledge to be able to function within the environment it wishes to operate in (Fratzke et al., 2019). The parties concerned should consider what policy and legal frameworks need to be established in order to create a sponsorship program.

Additionally, sponsorship programs require infrastructure in the form of "training and ongoing support for sponsors, public services that refugees can access when needed, and clear channels of communication between all parties involved in the resettlement and integration process" (Fratzke et al., 2019, p. 6). In the UK, for instance, the Reset charity was funded by the government to provide training for sponsors. Other examples of infrastructure needs are access to a country's public services for refugees (such as free language classes and employment services) (Fratzke et al., 2019).

A successful refugee sponsorship model also requires the necessary legal and financial means of providing effective and sustainable support. These investments and private funding would be best allocated to support sponsorship of developing information materials and trainings, the setup and operation of hotlines and central contact points, and creating sponsor networks for emotional support and peer learning (Fratzke et al., 2019).

The role of volunteers and sponsors who offer unique resources to complement the services of professional agencies and case workers should not be underestimated. While sponsors take on the responsibility for ensuring that newcomers achieve certain integration outcomes (such as acquiring stable housing or becoming self-sufficient), volunteers typically carry out discrete tasks or functions (such as teaching English) (Fratzke & Dorst, 2019). Policies with amplified investments in community engagement can lead to increases in refugees' access to individualized, ongoing support, which can further contribute to improved integration outcomes (Fratzke & Dorst, 2019). Several concrete policy recommendation that can contribute to more successful volunteer and sponsorship programs are as follows: (a) creating policy frameworks that allow agencies to engage volunteers or sponsors where they would add the most value; (b) designating funding for community engagement as part of the broader integration or resettlement strategy; and (c) providing a set of learning resources for agencies seeking to engage community members in service provision (Fratzke & Dorst, 2019).

Return and Reintegration Phenomenon

Return and reintegration policies are considered to be some of the most contentious types of migration policy (Newland & Salant, 2018). The manner in which individuals are returned could have critical financial, humanitarian, and development implications for the parties concerned depending on the methods chosen to execute these returns. The return spectrum of voluntariness includes solicited, voluntary, reluctant, pressured, obliged, and forced (Newland & Salant, 2018). When considering these returns, policy makers need to realize the complexities that each return migration strategy will bear. Return strategies present a level of complexities in dealing with frameworks. These include a need to maintain sovereignty over who enters or stays within the territory, a humanitarian obligation to tend to countries facing civil unrest or natural disasters, developmental impacts on the host country as well as the migrant country, reintegration assistance for migrants to benefit returning home countries, and a need to maintain a framework of stability and security (Newland & Salant, 2018).

While comprehensive data is limited as far as scale of return practices, some countries maintain records that may be useful in understanding the implications of various return/reintegration policies. Large-scale returns originating from the top ten countries of return tended to use forcible coercion to get enormous populations of migrants to return, and these programs often maintained few, if any, frameworks or safeguards (Newland & Salant, 2018). The most promising types of migrant return/reintegration programs consist of financial incentives and supportive measures (BMZ, 2018). For instance, the European Reintegration Network (ERIN) program provided individualized assistance for job placement; vocational training; and referrals to educational, legal, and psychological services. The intention of assistance-based programs is that migrants returning to their home countries will stimulate their home economies and add stability through their attained skills, education, and business ideas (European Reintegration Network, 2018). While in theory these programs help reintegrate and improve the economies of the migrant nation, the scale is small and fails to address the underlying structural issues that remain, such as lack of economic opportunity, corrupt governments, and violent conflicts (Newland & Salant, 2018).

Conclusions/Recommendations

This chapter revealed that policy analysts tend to typologize migration issues and provide recommendations based on the type of migration at stake. The sense-making claims often revolve around reasons why countries accept migrants: economic reasons drive labor migration policies, social reasons are reflected within family reunification policies, humanitarian reasons drive refugee and asylum seeker policies, and cultural and historical reasons appear within co-ethnics policies. When policy analysts discuss exclusion–inclusion claims, they are likely to appear within conversations on forcibly displaced people and how developed and developing nations address these groups. Our analysis brings us to a broad set of recommendations/lessons we learn from policy reports.

Lesson 1: Cooperation and Enhanced Partnerships

Cooperation and enhanced partnerships between origin and destination countries are of utmost importance (Bipartisan Policy Center, 2019; Blanchard, 2019; Doyle & Sharma, 2017; Hooper & Le Coz, 2020; Hugo, 2013; Khadria, 2017; Newland & Salant, 2018; O'Neil, 2003; Salvo & Barslund, 2020; Selee et al., 2019; Tamas, 2019, 2020). Most current migration policies can be considered a "one-sided game, that of the immigration country calling the shots," where "unilateral top-down policy decisions (are) devoid of willful, empathic or active involvement of the counterpart country or countries" (Khadria, 2017, p. 1). The dichotomy between the two complementary streams involved in migration (emigration and immigration) often leads to inconsistent, contradictory, and paradoxical positions between countries (Khadria, 2017). Even when migration partnerships between origin and destination countries do happen, they often focus on border enforcement and on incentives for countries of origin to prevent irregular migration. Much less is done to "address common concerns of origin countries, such as opening wider access for their nationals to legal migration pathways" (Newland, 2019, p. 6).

One example of a dialogue between states with a purpose to curb irregular and illegal migration is the EU's Mobility Partnerships. They are flexible, non-binding instruments that have a status of political declarations and a purpose of offering possible legal migration opportunities in exchange for fighting irregular migration (Tamas, 2019). Although these partnerships have taken a step toward more dialogue and cooperation (by substantially increasing destination countries' willingness to fund cooperation and make overall investments in origin countries' development), more needs to be done (Tamas, 2019). Simply discussing things that benefit the destination countries will not create that bond of mutual trust (Tamas, 2019). Analysts recommend adapting dialogue and cooperation alternatives to specific interests of diverse origin countries, upgrading these cooperation ideas on economic and social development to practice (not just at the rhetorical level), incorporating evidence-based research on drivers of migration, and progressing beyond smaller-scale pilot projects (Tamas, 2019).

Another recommendation is to take regional approach to migration, as broader regional cooperation is vital to comprehensively addressing the various forces driving irregular migration. That means engaging in ways that are mutually beneficial for all countries involved rather than seeking to impose unilateral measures that undermine cooperation (Selee et al., 2019). Additionally, policy analysts recognize that there is a heavy reliance on local governments during migration processes and that an emphasis on cooperation between federal and local governments is needed. For example, local governments are critical in the implementation of changes, recording of data, and relaying of information to migrants. Investment in regulations, staff, and infrastructure across multiple sectors will benefit migrants and local governments alike (Fratzke & Le Coz, 2019). This will increase the likelihood of local ownership if both parties benefit. Clearly defined coordination structures will also make it easier for agencies to enact change and for governments to properly implement protections for migrants.

Lesson 2: A Need for Comprehensive Policy That Integrates Development, Migration, and Foreign Policy Goals

Policy analysts maintain that the solution to current migration crises exists in global negotiations for policies to create sustainable developmental goals for migrant countries (Clemens & Postel, 2018; Hooper & Le Coz, 2020; Hooper & Newland, 2018; Hugo, 2013; Newland & Salant, 2018; Salvo & Barslund, 2020; Tamas, 2019, 2020). Thus, it is recommended that destination countries focus less on their own migration policies and look at opportunities to promote development within origin countries (Tamas, 2019). Negotiations are already within the works of creating a sustainable compromise in frameworks to uphold humanitarian needs, all the while allowing security, stability, and developmental solutions to counteract the loss of income through large-scale exit of migrants. Through careful coordination, countries can create policies that ensure greater stability to fix underlying issues, and host countries can equip migrants with the resources they need to become productive members of society (Newland & Salant, 2018). One such attempt is the concept of policy coherence for development (PCD) (Tamas, 2020), which incorporates three major goals: advancing shared objectives through synergies, minimizing negative side effects, and preventing policies from working at cross purposes (Hong & Knoll, 2016).

Policies that reduce costs of investments by migrants in their countries are often fruitless if there are not sufficient development opportunities for investments in the origin communities and countries (Hugo, 2013). Examples of policies that tie developmental and migration goals are in Australia and New Zealand, where national development agencies have invested in offering additional skills development opportunities for seasonal workers, with add-on training modules focused on helping migrants develop skills that can be put to use when they return home (Hooper & Le Coz, 2020). Successful integration of development and migration policies lies in "setting mutually agreed goals for cooperation that balance development and migration priorities and in establishing realistic expectations about the likely outcomes and the timeline for results" (Hooper & Newland, 2018, p. 9). The shared common priorities between two policy areas are within interventions in origin countries that relate to addressing barriers to economic growth; building resilience; promoting better reintegration outcomes; and facilitating skilled migration (Hooper & Newland, 2018).

It is important to note that simply increasing aid to developing countries will not result in less irregular and illegal migration. Quite to the contrary, economic development in low-income countries typically raises migration (Clemens & Postel, 2018). According to policy analysts that study "root causes" of migration, development aid can "only deter migration if it causes specific large changes in the countries migrants come from and those changes must cause fewer people to move" (Clemens & Postel, 2018, p. 1). There are key lessons for policy makers to consider when integrating development and migration policy goals. First, youth employment programs in poor countries can modestly reduce migration spikes in the short term (Clemens & Postel, 2018). Second, more information is needed to understand "root causes" of migration. An example of such a step is improved transparency and reporting on relevant aid programming, such as the precedent set by the OECD Creditor Monitoring System reporting of aid projects targeting environmental and gender inequality (Clemens & Postel, 2018). Additionally, rigorous experimentation and evaluation is much needed. An example of such an experiment is the research facilities created under the EU Africa Trust Fund (Clemens & Postel, 2018). Finally, the aid efforts aimed at shaping migration must look beyond deterrence, and agencies should, therefore, focus on cooperation with migrant-origin countries to shape how migration occurs (Clemens & Postel, 2018).

Further, some analysts recommend treating foreign policy as a form of migration policy (Clemens & Postel, 2017). As public resources are finite, making decisions as to where to provide foreign aid are of importance. Scholars argue that geographical and sectoral targeting of foreign assistance can greatly enhance complementarity with immigration policy (Clemens & Postel, 2017). As an example, they estimated that additional cost-effective investment in regional violence prevention in Central America during 2011 to 2016 could have substantially reduced the suffering and costs associated with unaccompanied child migration (Clemens & Postel, 2017).

Lesson 3: Development and Execution of Information Campaigns

Prevention and information campaigns in origin countries are successful in re-ducing irregular and illegal migration (Dumont et al., 2020). Illegal and irregu-lar migrants are often ill-informed and too easily influenced by rumors that are perpetuated by smuggling networks (Dumont et al., 2020). Debunking of these rumors and misinformation can help to reduce the risk that potential migrants are misled by unrealistic representations of life in destination countries. The use of credible sources (such as nonprofit and nongovernment organizations) can add to the credibility, as migrants often distrust official information (Dumont et al., 2020). Examples of such public information campaigns are the Migrar Informados (Informed Migration) campaign in Mexico, the Échale ganas (Go for it!) campaign in Guatemala, the Conectá con tu futuro (Connect with Your Future) campaign in El Salvador, and the Ponele plan a tu vida (Plan Your Life!) campaign in Honduras. They are focused on "encouraging young people to develop a life plan, be informed about the alternatives to irregular migration and understand the risks it entails" (IOM, 2020).

Some recommendations from policy analysts include highlighting the efforts and positive results occurring within origin countries and promoting confidence in local governance and civic action to support the ongoing efforts toward sta-bility and economic opportunities (Blanchard, 2019). Additionally, news of security improvements and anti-corruption efforts could be publicized. Some examples of incremental successes within the NT countries are the high lev-el of arrests by the International Commission against Impunity in Guatemala (CICIG) and El Salvador's 30% reduction in homicide rates in ten target munic-ipalities since 2015 (Blanchard, 2019). Another example of success is a coordi-nated effort between the Honduran government and the U.S. Central American Regional Security Initiative (CARSI), which includes enforcement training, youth employment, and investment in community leadership, which resulted in a cut in homicides by half in some of the most dangerous neighborhoods in San Pedro Sula (Runde et al., 2016).

Information campaigns might also be useful in changing public opinion re-garding migration. Currently, the public sees permanent legal relocation as "good" and temporary migration as "bad." Changing this public opinion will enable policy makers to implement programs furthering circular migration (Hugo, 2013), which will contribute to safe, orderly, and Regular Migration (the aim of the Global Compact for Migration) and reduce irregular and illegal migration. Efforts to reduce the narrative of migrants as threats are also rec-ommended. Analysts argue that the de-humanizing public rhetoric surrounding those that are fleeing violence in their home countries is prevalent (Blanchard, 2019). Concerted efforts to change perceptions of refugees so that they are seen as rights-holders, contributors, and partners in the development of communities are of importance (Runde et al., 2018).

Lesson 4: Replacing Illegal and Irregular Migration with Regular Migration

Policy analysts strongly argue for policies that promote regular and legal migra-tion in an effort to replace illegal and irregular migration patterns (Khadria, 2017; Newland, 2017; Selee et al., 2019; United Nations, 2018). A mix of strategies can accomplish this goal: expanding existing legal pathways or creating new ones, reforming asylum systems, enhancing border control, and addressing the root causes of migration (Selee et al., 2019). It is impossible to overestimate that the enforcement alone, even if strengthened in both destination and origin countries, will dissuade irregular migration in a sustainable way (Selee et al., 2019).

Enabling mobility is one solution for replacing illegal and irregular migration with Regular Migration. The ease of travel in and out of the destination country is associated with more circular migration over permanent settlement (Hugo, 2013). Destination countries should focus on encouraging and facilitating cir-cular migration by keeping transaction costs to a minimum (Hugo, 2013).

Lesson 5: Increasing Administrative Capacity

Proper management and governance are key in the migration process. For example, in the case of asylum and refugee migration, it is important to for court systems to operate smoothly in order to provide timely and fair decisions (Hinojosa & Meyer, 2019). Reforming the asylum systems will enable timely decision-making that would ensure that those who qualify receive protection quickly and discourage the filing of less robust claims (Selee et al., 2019). No-tably, policies that limit access to asylum (such as forcing those seeking asylum to wait in neighboring countries, as in the case of the US and Mexico) are like-ly to backfire by strengthening smuggling networks and encouraging irregular crossings (Selee et al., 2019). Additionally, UNHCR efforts are insufficient in addressing asylum and refugee migration issues, and countries (both origin and destination) need to commit their own resources to build up their own refugee agencies (Meyer & Isacson, 2019). Strong oversight and accountability measures are also of major importance (Meyer & Isacson, 2019).

Lesson 6: Keeping Migration Policy Current and Fact Based

Governments should pay close attention to migration issues within their countries and update migration policies frequently. Legal and policy frameworks need to focus on the real-life issues that migrants are facing (Noack et al., 2020). For example, current US migration policies are outdated (Bipartisan Policy Center, 2019), as they were designed to reflect a different migration era—the one where most unauthorized immigrants were single, adult men from Mexico (Selee et al., 2019). A current assessment of policy needs will instantly reveal that the US needs to revisit the physical infrastructure for detention centers, career paths within border agencies, and the structure of ports of entry (Selee et al., 2019). These changes would help improve legal transit and commerce while responding more effectively to mixed flows of humanitarian and other migrants, and especially the needs of families and unaccompanied minors (Selee et al., 2019).

Additionally, policy makers should encourage fact-based migration policy (Blanchard, 2019). As an example, scholars have done extensive research and found that immigration and criminality are not linked in the first generation migrating to the US, but this information is often disregarded (Blanchard, 2019). Instead, the public discourse is centered on the threat of arrival of migrants and connections to violent crime (Blanchard, 2019).

The lack of up-to-date and comparable data on migration has been documented by policy analysts (Salvo & Barslund, 2020). It hinders the ability to make detailed analysis of policy issues, weakens the decision-making process, and, as a result, deteriorates the quality of policy response (Salvo & Barslund, 2020). The goal of collecting and utilizing accurate and disaggregated data to inform policy is also listed among the objectives of the Global Compact for Safe, Orderly and Regular Migration. A "migration policy scoreboard" has been suggested as a monitoring framework, which will match the complexity of migration while also accounting for the variations and differences among the countries (Salvo & Barslund, 2020, p. 4).

REFERENCES

Bertossi, C., & Duyvendak, J. W. (2012, July). National models of immigrant integration: The costs for comparative research. *Comparative European Politics*, *10*, 237–247. https://doi.org/10.1057/cep.2012.10

Bipartisan Policy Center. (2019). *Policy proposals to address the Central American migration challenge*. https://bipartisanpolicy.org/report/policy-proposals-to-address-the-central-american-migration-challenge/

Blanchard, D. N. (2019). *Immigration and national security: An empirical assessment of Central American immigration and violent crime in the United States* (Vol. 16). https://justiceinmexico.org/wp-content/uploads/2019/01/BLANCHARD_Immigration-and-National-Security.pdf

BMZ. (2018). *Voluntary return and re-integration—with prospects: The returnee program 'Returning to New Opportunities'*. Berlin. https://www.swp-berlin.org/10.18449/2019C40/

Brubaker, R. (1992). *Citizenship and nationhood in France and Germany*. Harvard University Press.

Brücker, H., Jaschke, P., & Kosyakova, Y. (2019). Integrating refugees and asylum seekers into the German economy and society: empirical evidence and policy objectives. *Washington (DC): Migra-tion Policy Institute*.

Clemens, M. (2015). Global Skill Partnerships: A proposal for technical training in a mobile world. *IZA Journal of Labor Policy*, *4*(1), 2. https://doi.org/10.1186/s40173-014-0028-z

Clemens, M., & Gough, K. (2017). Global Skill Partnerships: A Proposal for Technical Training in Settings of Forced Displacement. *Center for Global Development, Brief 2017*.

Clemens, M., Dempster, H., & Gough, K. (2019, October 24). *Promoting new kinds of legal labour migration pathways between Europe and Africa*. Center for Global Development. https://esa.un.org/unpd/wpp/Publications/Files/WPP2017_KeyFindings.pdf

Clemens, M., & Postel, H. M. (2017, September). *Foreign policy is migration policy: Lessons from the drivers of Central American child migration* (pp. 1–4). Center for Global Development.

Clemens, M., & Postel, H. M. (2018). *Can development assistance deter emigration?* Center for Global Development. https://www.cgdev.org/publication/can-development-assistance-deter-emigration

Commission of the European Communities. (2005, December). *Policy plan on legal migration* (p. 29). http://aei.pitt.edu/37800/

Corrado, A. (2017). Migrant crop pickers in Italy and Spain. *Heinrich Böll Foundation: Berlin, Germany*, 1-23.

Doyle, J. J. G., & Sharma, M. (2017). *Maximizing the development impacts from temporary migration*. World Bank Group. https://doi.org/10.1596/29622

Dumont, J.-C., Chaloff, J., & Liebig, T. (2020). *What are the possible policy responses to future irregular migration ?* Policy Commons. https://policycommons.net/artifacts/3797995/what-are-the-possible-policy-responses-to-future-irregular-migration/4603823/

European Reintegration Network. (2018). *ERIN specific action program: Afghanistan.* ERIN. https://docplayer.net/57714087 -European-reintegration-network-erin-specific-action-program -afghanistan-briefing-note.html

Felter, C. (2019). *U.S. temporary foreign worker programs. Council on foreign relations.* https://www.cfr.org/backgrounder/us-temporary -foreign-worker-programs

Finotelli, C., & Michalowski, I. (2012). The heuristic potential of models of citizenship and immigrant integration reviewed. *Journal of Immigrant and Refugee Studies*, *10*(3), 231–240. https://doi.org/10.108 0/15562948.2012.693033

Fratzke, S., & Dorst, E. (2019, November). *Volunteers and sponsors: A catalyst for refugee integration?* Transatlantic Council on Migration. https://www.migrationpolicy.org/research/volunteers-sponsors-refugee-integration

Fratzke, S., Kainz, L., Beirens, H., Dorst, E., & Bolter, J. (2019). *Refugee sponsorship programs: A global state of play and opportunities for investment. Migration Policy Institute Europe*, (15), 1–21.

Fratzke, S., & Le Coz, C. (2019). Strengthening refugee protection in low- and middle-income countries. *Migration Policy Institute*, (7), 1–24. https://www.migrationpolicy.org/sites/default/files/publications /MPI-StrengtheningRefugeeProtection_Final.pdf

Gibson, J., & McKenzie, D. (2014). Development through seasonal worker programs: The case of New Zealand's RSE program. In *International handbook on migration and economic development* (pp. 186–210). https://doi.org/10.4337/9781782548072.00011

Greenberg, M., Gelatt, J., Bolter, J., Workie, E., & Charo, I. (2018, December). *Promoting refugee integration in challenging times: The potential of two-generation strategies*. Migration Policy Institute. https://www.migrationpolicy.org/research/refugee-integration-two-generation-strategies

Hedberg, C., Axelsson, L., & Abella, M. (2019). *Thai Berry Pickers in Sweden: A migration corridor to a low wage sector*. UMEÅ University. https://umu.diva-portal.org/smash/record.jsf?pid=diva2%3A1322935&dswid=-3709

Helbling, M., & Vink, M. P. (2013, September). The use and misuse of policy indices in the domain of citizenship and integration. *Comparative European Politics*, 11, 551–554. https://doi.org/10.1057/cep.2013.10

Hinojosa, G., & Meyer, M. (2019). *Protecting refugees and restoring order: Real solutions to the humanitarian crisis*. https://www.wola.org/analysis/human-rights-policy-solutions-central-american-humanitarian-crisis/

Hong, A., & Knoll, A. (2016). *Strengthening the migration-development nexus through improved policy and institutional coherence*. www.KNOMAD.org

Hooper, K. (2019). Reimagining skilled migration partnerships to support development. *Migration Policy Institute*, 1–24. www.migrationpolicy.org/sites/default/files/publications/GlobalCompact-SkillPartnerships_FinalWeb.pdf

Hooper, K., & Le Coz, C. (2020, February). *Seasonal worker programmes in Europe: Promising practices and ongoing challenges*. Migration Policy Institute Europe.

Hooper, K., & Newland, K. (2018, July). *Mind the gap: Bringing migration into development partnerships and vice versa*. Migration Policy Institute.

Huang, C., Charles, S., Post, L., & Gough, K. (2018, April). *Tackling the realities of protracted displacement case studies on what's working and where we can do better*. Center for Global Development. www.cgdev.org/sites/default/files/tackling-realities-protracted-displacement-case-studies-whats-working.pdf

Huang, C., & Graham, J. (2018). *Are refugees located near urban job opportunities? An analysis of overlap between refugees and major urban areas in developing countries, and implications for employment opportunities and engagement*. Center for Global Development.

Hudson, N. F. (2020). *Intra-corporate transferees (ICTs): The benefits for the EU and the opportunity cost*. www.peacebuilding.no

Hugo, G. (2013). *What we know about circular migration and enhanced mobility*. Migration Policy Institute. https://www.migrationpolicy.org/research /what-we-know-about-circular-migration-and-enhanced-mobility

IOM. (2020, February 21). *IOM campaigns help communities in Mexico and Central America seek alternatives to irregular migration*. International Organization for Migration. https://www.iom.int/news/iom-campaigns-help-commu-nities-mexico-and-central-america-seek-alternatives-irregular-migration

Jordan, M. (2015). Visa glitch stalls workers, straining U.S. farms. *The Wall Street Journal*. https://www.wsj.com/articles/visa-glitch-stalls-workers -straining-u-s-farms-1434411601

Khadria, B. (2017). In Each Other's Shoes: Making Migration Policies Equi-table Across Borders'. *Migration Research Leaders' Syndicate: Ideas to Inform International Cooperation on Safe, Orderly and Regular Migration*, 49-54.

Koopmans, R. (2013). Indices of immigrant rights: What have we learned, where should we go? *Comparative European Politics*, *11*(5), 696–703. https:// doi.org/10.1057/cep.2013.17

Koopmans, R., Statham, P., Giugni, M., & Passy, F. (2005). *Contested citizenship* (Vol. 25). University of Minnesota Press. http://www.jstor.org /stable/10.5749/j.ctttsd0w

Meissner, D. (2019). *Rethinking U.S. immigration policy: New realities call for new answers*. Migration Policy Institute. https://www.migrationpolicy.org /research/rethinking-us-immigration-policy-new-realities-call-new-answers

Meissner, D., Hipsman, F., & Aleinikoff, T. A. (2018). *The U.S. asylum sys-tem in crisis: Charting a way forward*. Migration Policy Institute. https://www .migrationpolicy.org/research/us-asylum-system-crisis-charting-way-forward

Meyer, M., & Isacson, A. (2019). *The "Wall" before the wall: Mexi-co's crackdown on migration at its southern border*. https://www.wola.org /analysis/wola-report-mexicos-southern-border-security-central-american -migration-u-s-policy/

Munck, G. L., & Verkuilen, J. (2002, February). Conceptualizing and mea-suring democracy: Evaluating alternative indices. *Comparative Political Stud-ies*, *35*(1). https://doi.org/10.1177/001041400203500101

Natter, K. (2015). *Revolution and political transition in Tunisia: A migration game changer?* Migration Policy Institute. https://www.migrationpolicy.org /article/revolution-and-political-transition-tunisia-migration-game-changer

Newland, K. (2017, November). *The global compact for migration: How does development fit in?* (pp. 1–14). Migration Policy Institute.

Newland, K. (2019, June). *Migration, development, and global governance.* Migration Policy Institute.

Newland, K., & Riester, A. (2018). *Welcome to work? Legal migration pathways for low-skilled workers.* Migration Policy Institute.

Newland, K., & Salant, B. (2018, October). Balancing acts: Policy frameworks for migrant return and reintegration. Migration Policy Institute.

Nibbs, F. G. (2016). *Moving Into the Fastlane: Understanding refugee upward mobility in the context of resettlement.* Forced Migration Upward Mobility Project.

Noack, M., Wagner, M., & Jacobs, C. (2020). *Governing protracted displacement what access to solutions for forcibly displaced people?* Creative Commons. https://www.ssoar.info/ssoar/handle/document/68882

O'Neil, K. (2003). *Discussion on migration and development: Using remittances and circular migration as drivers for development.* https://www.migrationpolicy.org/research/discussion-migration-and-development-using-remittances-and-circular-migration-drivers

Pressestelle, G. (2017, July 31). *Attracting qualified nurses to Germany: Federal employment agency and GIZ recruit one-thousandth nurse from partner countries.* https://www.giz.de/en/press/55916.html

Runde, D., Perkins, C., & Nealer, E. (2016). *Achieving growth and security in the northern triangle of Central America.* www.rowman.com

Runde, D., Yayboke, E. K., & Milner, A. N. (2018). *Confronting the global forced migration crisis.*Center for Strategic & International Studies. https://www.csis.org/analysis/confronting-global-forced-migration-crisis

Safran, W. (1997). Citizenship and nationality in democratic systems: Approaches to defining and acquiring membership in the political community. *International Political Science Review/Revue Internationale de Science Politique, 18*(3), 313–335. http://www.jstor.org/stable/1601346

Salvo, M. D., & Barslund, M. (2020). *Migration policy scoreboard: A monitoring mechanism for EU Asylum and migration policy.* https://cadmus.eui.eu/bitstream/handle/1814/66528/PB_2020_11_MPC.pdf?sequence=1&isAllowed=y Schmid, S. D., & Helbling, M. (2016).

Validating the immigration policies in comparison (IMPIC) dataset. WZB Berlin Social Science Center (SP VI 2016–202), 1–35. www.wzb .eu

Selee, A., Giorguli-Saucedo, S. E., Soto, A. G. R., & Masferrer, C. (2019, September). *Investing in the neighborhood: Changing Mexico-U.S. Migration patterns and opportunities for sustainable cooperation.* Migration Policy Institute. https://www.migrationpolicy.org/research /mexico-us-migration-opportunities-sustainable-cooperation

Tamas, K. (2019). *Assessing the EU's external migration policy.* Prague Process.   https://www.pragueprocess.eu/en/migration-observatory /publications/34-briefs/196-assessing-the-eu-s-external-migration-policy

Tamas, K. (2020). *Making the EU's migration and development policies more coherent.* Prague Process. https://www.pragueprocess.eu/en /news-events/news/370-making-the-eu-s-migration-and-development -policies-more-coherent

UN General Assembly. (2006). *International migration and development: Report of the secretary-general.* https://www.refworld.org/docid /44ca2d934.html

UNHCR. (2018, June 25). Global trends: Forced displacement in 2017. *Global Trends, 76.* https://migrantprotection.iom.int/en/resources/reports/ global-trends-forced-displacement-2017#:~:text=Globally%2C%20 the%20forcibly%20displaced%20population,%2C%20conflict%2C%20 or%20generalized%20violence.

UNHCR. (2020). *UNHCR figures at a glance.* https://www.unhcr.org /figures-at-a-glance.html

United Nations. (2018). *Global compact for safe, orderly and regular migration.* https://refugeesmigrants.un.org/sites/default/files/180713 _agreed_outcome_global_compact_for_migration.pdf

Wheels24. (2019, May 7). Proud day for SA graduates of cross-brand social vocational education training for Porsche. *Wheels24.* https://www .wheels24.co.za/News/proud-day-for-sa-graduates-of-cross-brand -social-vocational-education-training-for-porsche-20190705

## CHAPTER 7

Narrative Alignment

Multifaceted issues tend to be some of the hardest challenges to face when different stakeholders focus narrowly on a small subset of the whole issue. This is even more problematic when stakeholders then spin public narratives to inform policy decisions based on less complete and even false narratives. The result is a zero-sum issue that ignores important narratives because they don't fit into an agenda. Ultimately, the consequence is less effective policy and a subsequent decrease in confidence in democracy (Jones & McBeth, 2020). With a subject as multifaceted as migration across the southern US border, we see a prime example of this as policy decisions based on incomplete narratives can vacillate dramatically from one polar opposite to another (Estrada et al., 2020).

This study was designed to look at the issue from the vantage of multiple stakeholders. We generally categorized the stakeholders into three broad groups: policy makers, media reports, and individuals with ties to migration. Policy briefs were used to identify policy narratives. Media reports from the many affected countries were analyzed to identify narratives used in the media. Finally, depth interviews with individual stakeholders were invaluable to shed light on potentially missing narratives from other areas studied. The individuals interviewed included policy makers, journalists, law enforcement workers, academics who study migration, shelter workers, and actual migrants. Analyzing these varied narratives illuminated areas where the narratives are aligned. Rather than attempting to construct our own narrative of migration, this work examines the limits on which migration is creatively imagined within the scope of currently available narratives, specifically attempting to highlight the distinctions and areas of alignment between those narratives. Doing so brought to light several areas of alignment.

Narrative Alignment 1: Migrants Are Seeking a Better Life

While this might seem like a very simple observation, cooperation and enhanced partnerships between origin and destination countries are of utmost importance (Bipartisan Policy Center, 2019; Blanchard, 2019; Doyle & Sharma, 2017; Hooper & Le Coz, 2020; Hugo, 2013; Khadria, 2017; Newland & Salant, 2018; O'Neil, 2003; Salvo & Barslund, 2020; Selee et al., 2019; Tamas, 2019, 2020). Most of the current migration policies can be considered a "one-sided game, that of the immigration country calling the shots," where "unilateral top-down policy decisions (are) devoid of willful, empathic or active involvement of the counterpart country or countries" (Khadria, 2017, p. 1). The dichotomy between the two complementary streams involved in migration (emigration and immigration) often leads to inconsistent, contradictory, and paradoxical positions between countries (Khadria, 2017). Even when migration partnerships between origin and destination countries do happen, they often focus on border enforcement and on incentives for countries of origin to prevent irregular migration. Much less is done to "address common concerns of origin countries, such as opening wider access for their nationals to legal migration pathways" (Newland, 2019, p. 6).

Various sources agree that the general reasons for forced migration from Northern Triangle countries toward the US include violence and corruption at home, gang and criminal activity disrupting neighborhoods, reports (often from family and friends) of better opportunities in the US and, to a lesser extent, lack of gainful employment in the home country. It is also important to note that one other reason for migration is environmental impacts on traditional agricultural industry, such as drought, floods, or other extreme weather destroying crops and land needed to survive and earn a living. These conditions leave many residents without a way to provide for loved ones and desperate to find a solution—with a lack of help coming from any other source. This reason surfaced frequently among migrants and those who interact with migrants. That narrative appears less frequently in policy briefs but is almost nonexistent in media reports. Media reports do cover many extreme weather events but rarely focus on impact on the well-being of people struggling to make ends meet.

The result is quite a bit of narrative alignment on most of the causes of forced migration but very little on the severity of the problem and almost nothing on options migrants have when being forced to migrate. Sadly, migrants interviewed told heart-wrenching stories of gangs threatening to kidnap young daughters and sell them into the sex trade if families didn't pay protection money. Young boys were being told they had to join the violent gangs or families would be harmed. With no support from local law enforcement, often controlled by the gangs as well, families were forced to flee.

It is clear that narratives are aligned in describing reasons why migrants are forced to migrate.

Narrative Alignment 2: The Migration Journey Is Perilous

The journey of a migrant through Central America and Mexico and across the US border, ultimately to settle somewhere within the US is a perilous one. This is clearly an area of narrative alignment across the various sources studied in this research. Weather-related perils, violence, poor shelter options, and lack of food and water are just the beginning. Mexican media and shelter workers all confirm the narrative that the journey is dangerous. US media and stakeholders confirm that getting across the US border is also perilous. At every point along the journey, migrants are vulnerable.

In Mexico, shelter workers report limited capacity to host migrants. Shelters also have to deal with lack of funding from host countries and other donors. These same shelters must also weed out legitimate migrants from criminals and gang members making the journey. As a result, deaths are frequent along the path of migration. This narrative features in nearly every interview or report examined for this study. Interviews and Mexican media occasionally report efforts to create a favorable environment for migrants to remain in Mexico—ending the migration early. But as a result of changes in funding from different leaders in power, these programs tend to be inconsistent and ineffective in achieving any lasting impact.

Similarly, reports are aligned in the US about efforts to help migrants who arrive to transition into a stable life. Interviews with academics and other stakeholders have shown that funding dries up with changes in US government administrations. Media and other narratives are frequently hostile to migrants who live in fear of being sent back to some point along the migration path with no means of supporting themselves.

Ultimately, while the narrative of a perilous migration journey exists across all stakeholders, it is often limited to the region the stakeholder operates within. Migrants themselves (and to some extent academics) tend to be the only stakeholders who can elaborate on the peril of the entire journey. When crafting cohesive policy, therefore, it is important for stakeholders to collaborate with other stakeholders in order to evolve a comprehensive and collaborative policy to address both the causes of migration and the dangers of the journey itself.

Narrative Alignment 3: The US Migration Infrastructure and Policy Have Not Been Able to Either Deter Migration or Facilitate Efficient Legal Migration

Along with the causes of forced migration, and the dangers of the journey, one other area of complete alignment in the narrative among all stakeholders emerged. It is clear that the US migration infrastructure and policy have been insufficient to deter irregular migration. What is also beyond dispute is that the avenues for legal migration are overwhelmed or simply inaccessible for the majority of forced migrants. As priorities change from administration to administration, the emphasis has shifted between polar opposite policies. One policy would seek to keep everyone out of the US and round up anyone who arrived irregularly and ship them out—often with little care about the conditions those migrants will find when sent back. The other policy seemingly results in multitudes of migrants flocking to the border due to a perceived reduction in hostility toward migrants.

Narratives agree that pathways for legal migration are limited. First, they are costly and take years to work out. Second, there is a clear narrative about insufficient numbers of immigration judges to handle legal petitions. Finally, the conditions on which a migrant could claim asylum or refugee status require such a high level of documentation that hitting that level becomes next to impossible for a migrant to prove.

Finally, resources are not available to the extent that would be required for any type of migrant to transition into productive life inside the US. Certain administrations will allocate more or fewer resources to these agencies based on the political narrative they support.

The result of this policy vacillation has been widely reported in an incomplete border wall, overwhelmed detention centers for captured migrants, varying policies about separation of families and children, and the empowerment of cartels and gangs who become the only entities with the means to transport people (and other illicit items) across the border.

Conclusions

Key Elements of the Northern Triangle Migration Narrative

This study sought to provide a more comprehensive perspective on the issue of irregular Northern Triangle migration and its implications for US policy framing. Using a narrative framework to understand how the US, Mexico, and Northern Triangle (NT) nations understand the problems, causes, and perceptions of each other's actions in respect to migration can allow for substantive shifts in behavior toward more cooperative efforts to combat illegal migration and its humanitarian consequences.

Drawing from interview data, policy proposals, and media coverage related to migration, the findings show that the US migration system and its asylum-claim policies are ill-equipped and overwhelmed by the flow of NT migrants. US societal recognition of the complexities surrounding migration have developed slowly, and the issue of migration has been detrimentally politicized.

The analysis of data collected in this report evidences a narrative portrait of NT migration as incentivized by gang and political violence, economic inequality, corruption facilitated in transit by dangerous criminal smuggling networks profiting from stringent enforcement of anti-migration policies carried out by government officials.

Taking a narrative view, comprised of scenes, acts, agents, instruments, and purpose, of how migration is understood from the data sources of the study, the following insights are evident:

> The scene in which migration occurs appears largely undisputed: over the past two decades, increasing numbers of migrants are embarking on a journey to the US. In doing so, migrants suffer from significant humanitarian abuse, violence, family separation, and loss of life.
>
> On reaching the US border, US immigration officials are overwhelmed, understaffed, and ill-equipped—lacking the time and resources to handle the volume of people and their needs; driving perceptions, and exacerbating the reality, of migrants being treated in an undignified, inhumane manner.

A key scenic element missing from US considerations is the root causes of the migration journey, that is, escaping poverty and violence experienced within their country of origin.

The actions most frequently referenced in respect to migration reveal numerous commonalities across stakeholders and national media systems. The most commonly mentioned "acts" include migrants leaving their homes to travel to the US, the experiences of detentions, deportations, family separations, and violence committed against migrants while on the migratory journey. Unfortunately, these reported acts seemingly dominate narratives on migration, with discussions in the US, in particular, focused on deterrent actions and enforcement. This action-oriented focus draws attention to the immediate present, while obscuring the longer term consequences and deeper causes of irregular migration.

While key agents include government agencies, such as US and Mexican immigration officials charged with implementing deportation-related policies, only recently has the US begun to realize that NT migrants are the primary agents embarking on the migratory journey. Other emerging agents include criminal organizations, specifically drug cartels, who financially profit and monopolize the routes through Mexico to the US, as well as illegal entry into US territory.

There has also been a shift in migrant demographics from single, largely male, Mexican laborers to Central American families, specifically, women and children, that blurs clear-cut categorizations. US mentality regarding the changing nature of those migrating has been slow to shift, with larger societal views of immigration still representing migrants as simply Mexicans seeking labor.

Taken together, the largest divergence in US, Mexican, and NT societies' understanding of migration are underlying push/pull factors leading migrants to come to the US—and the instruments or means by which they do so—leading to a lack of understanding of US migration policies blocking migrant entry. Thus, whereas US discourse on migration has increasingly solidified into a discussion on "border security," NT and Mexican discourses emphasize the humanitarian need to seek a better life, including economic opportunity, as well as a life free from overt violence. While the right to protect one's border has some resonance with Mexican and NT perspectives on migration, the US' preoccupation with border security is seen as inappropriately criminalizing migration, ignoring the plight of migrants in ways that empower criminal organizations. A common plotline is that US border enforcement policies work only to push migrants into increasingly dangerous illegal pathways to reach the US. While the migrants themselves are not seen as criminals, the process of migration now inherently involves close contact with criminal organizations, human smugglers, and life-threatening circumstances. The relational linkage of migration, and migrants, to harrowing criminal enterprise helps fuel demonizing rhetoric and negatively impacts support for US policies aimed at humanitarian relief. Consequently, US officials, and their actions, are described as treating migrants in an undignified manner, robbing migrants of their humanity. As noted previously, many potential interviewees contacted for this study refused participation, citing distrust and disgust with the US Department of Homeland Security as their reasoning.

Opportunities for US-Led Policy Narratives on Migration

Despite grim presentations of migration and its processes, there are tangible actions US officials can take to reframe the broader narratives concerning NT migration around longer term solutions and visions. The data shows the US has significant capacity for moral leadership and the resources to enact change in a more efficacious manner, if it chooses to do so.

In sum, US policy narratives should focus on the common motivations of migrants, as well as those of transit and destination countries. A commonality across the data is the desire to stem the destabilizing effects of migration. Societies, at their core, strive to provide conditions for individuals to live prosperous lives and to avoid inhumane treatment of those seeking prosperity. Stories framing migratory acts as illegal or focused on US deterrence policies spiral into conflict-laden binaries and should be avoided. Such presentations conflate criminality and migration in ways that neglect NT and Mexican perspectives on US policies and push antagonistic frames of migrants as illegal, unwanted, and burdensome to societies.

Furthermore, offering narratives that educate audiences on the motivations for, and processes deleterious to, migration—crippling violence, corruption, failing institutions, lack of land access, climate change, rampant criminal enterprises of human smuggling, economic disparities, lack of opportunities, overwhelmed border resources, dated asylum-seeking processes, inadequate assimilation infrastructure—can provide a common starting point undergirding the overarching purpose of migration policy. With a common outlined purpose, policy narratives can shift from insular concerns to cooperative goals of burden-sharing across nations.

More specifically, the findings from our study suggest the following approaches to US narrative presentation of migration from the NT to include:

Employing messages that explain how US policies address the root causes of migration.

- Outline push/pull factors such as violence and instability, corruption, degraded government capacities, economic issues. Vocal stances against corruption from US leaders are important.
- Describe how policies can create pockets of stability across NT and Mexico; particularly meaningful focuses are indigenous empowerment (land access, direct involvement in planning of relief and assistance efforts, skill and trade development) and cooperative partnering with NGOs already offering services and assistance to targeted areas.
- Recognize that current US policies and restrictions incentivize criminal cartel control of human smuggling to the US, weakening anti-corruption efforts in the NT and eroding confidence in cooperative solutions.

Reclaim moral high ground through transcendent narratives of multilateral cooperation.

- US rhetoric on migration should adjust toward describing humanitarian efforts, both at the border and in transit-origin countries, rather than focusing on criminality and the desperate acts of migrants.
- Recognize that US security-based rhetoric emphasizing restrictions and deterrence efforts allows human smugglers and cartels to spread disinformation that creates surges in crossing attempts.
- Present migration as an international issue of combating corruption and criminal organizations.
- Use rhetoric that ingratiates active regional and international NGOs, as well as other states capable of burden-sharing (i.e., Canada, Costa Rica, Panama).

Re-characterize migrants and avoid language criminalizing migration.

- Humanize migrants by describing their plight as one in search of basic human dignity and safety.

- Capitalize on terminology already meaningful within migrant communities, such as "New American."
- Re-contextualize migration by describing its historical roots and recognize it as a naturally occurring, cyclical human phenomenon unalterable by defensive solutions alone to reduce fear of migration.
- Highlight the contributions and entrepreneurial initiatives of migrants and migrant communities in the US and transit countries.

Provide narrative messaging clarifying the US migration processes.

- Reframe US migration process as a transparent, rule of law approach emphasizing fairness. Migrants are misinformed and unprepared when seeking asylum, resulting in further case backlogs, overrun detention facilities, and incentivizing the use of human smugglers. Explaining asylum rules and investing in partnerships with civil society actors and multilateral institutions already aiding asylum seekers can help mitigate problems.
- Explain the adjudication processes in ways that individuals can prepare and facilitate proof of identity. Clear adjudication guidelines give migrants who are turned away a sense of fairness and dignity.
- Open pathways for asylum seekers to receive an explanation of the process and to present their case for asylum in their native language.
- Recognize that a lack of trained social workers along with underfunded, overcrowded US detention facilities undermines faith in legal immigration processes and asylum seeking, perpetuating narratives promoting illegal migration through human smugglers and criminal organizations.
- Recognize that US information campaigns must continuously evolve to reflect the dynamic nature of immigration. Migrants focus largely on positive exemplars; inconsistent and unclear US policies foster false hopes. Instead, informational campaigns explaining qualifications for asylum can provide transparency to set realistic expectations, specifically by linking such efforts with transnational institutions and civil society actors to leverage existing networks and boost messaging credibility.

Avoid politicizing the issue of migration.

- Avoid emotionally charged terms demonizing or criminalizing migration; such rhetoric polarizes US society and draws attention to actions deterring

migration rather than those addressing root causes and associated humanitarian issues.

- Narrative themes like "fortress America" or "migrants as criminals" or "stealing of US jobs" present wedge issues undermining US ability to enact policies and make investments addressing the root causes of migration.

Demonstrate help to those already here.

- Foster greater appreciation for migrants within the US, and provide visible backing of reform measures needed to address US system vocational and documentation-oriented barriers (e.g., driver's license, bank account) that marginalize migrants or force them into the shadows of society. Reducing the negative stigmas surrounding migration can foster novel solutions to problems, as more parties are willing to engage in the discussion.
- Create discussions that weave community partners together with migrants to offer localized vocational training and opportunities.
- Interview data and media reports both suggest migrants face difficulties when assimilating in the US. How a problem is understood, or a situation defined, implicates the conceivable solutions open for pursuit. In this sense, how we talk about migration can, over time, reorient actions and outcomes. By considering the perspective of others in relation to one's own, we open up the possibility for change. Outlining a narrative perspective of how US, NT, and Mexican audiences make sense of transnational migration from the NT emphasizes the communicative dynamics of migration policies, offering a broad picture from which to begin comprehending scope. Having such a perspective is a first step toward shifting how US agencies talk about migration, both in external messages as well as in formulating policies that enable meaningful cooperative solutions.

REFERENCES

Bipartisan Policy Center. (2019). *Policy proposals to address the Central American migration challenge.* https://bipartisanpolicy.org/report/policy-pro-posals-to-address-the-central-american-migration-challenge/

Blanchard, D. N. (2019). *Immigration and national security : An empirical assessment of Central American immigration and violent crime in the United States* (Vol. 16). www.justiceinmexico.org

Doyle, J. J. G., & Sharma, M. (2017). *Maximizing the development impacts from temporary migration.* World Bank Group.

Estrada, E. P., Ebert, K., & Liao, W. (2020). Polarized toward apathy: An analysis of the privatized immigration-control debate in the trump era. *PS: Political Science & Politics, 53*(4), 679-684.

Hooper, K., & Le Coz, C. (2020, February). *Seasonal worker programmes in Europe: Promising practices and ongoing challenges.* Migration Policy Institute Europe.

Hugo, G. (2013). What we know about circular migration and enhanced mobility. *Migration Policy Institute Policy Brief,* (7). https://www.migrationpolicy. org/research/what-we-know-about-circular-migration-and-enhanced-mobility

Jones, M. D., & McBeth, M. K. (2020). Narrative in the Time of Trump: Is the Narrative Policy Framework good enough to be relevant?. *Administrative Theory & Praxis, 42*(2), 91-110.

Newland, K. (2019, June). *Migration, development, and global governance.* Migration Policy Institute.

Newland, K., & Salant, B. (2018, October). *Balancing acts: Policy frameworks for migrant return and reintegration.* Migration Policy Institute.

O'Neil, K. (2003). *Discussion on migration and development : Using remittances and circular migration as drivers for development.* https://www .migrationpolicy.org/research/discussion-migration-and-development-using -remittances-and-circular-migration-drivers

Selee, A., Giorguli-Saucedo, S. E., Soto, A. G. R., & Masferrer, C. (2019, September). *Investing in the neighborhood: Changing Mexico-U.S. Migration patterns and opportunities for sustainable cooperation.* Migration Policy Institute. https://www.migrationpolicy.org/research/mexico-us-migration-opportu nities-sustainable-cooperation

Tamas, K. (2019). *Assessing the EU's external migration policy.* Prague Process. https://www.pragueprocess.eu/en/migration-observatory/publications /34-briefs/196-assessing-the-eu-s-external-migration-policy

Tamas, K. (2020). *Making the EU's migration and development policies more coherent.* Prague Process. https://www.pragueprocess.eu/en/news- events/news/370-making-the-eu-s-migration-and-development-policies-more -coherent

www.ingramcontent.com/pod-product-compliance
Lightning Source LLC
Chambersburg PA
CBHW031550260326
41914CB00002B/355